ALSO BY SARAH VOWELL

Radio On: A Listener's Diary

Take the Cannoli

[Stories from the New World]

SARAH VOWELL

SIMON & SCHUSTER

NEW YORK LONDON TORONTO SYDNEY SINGAPORE

SIMON & SCHUSTER

Rockefeller Center

1230 Avenue of the Americas

New York, NY 10020

DESIGNED BY JILL WEBER

Manufactured in the United States of America

3   5   7   9   10   8   6   4   2

LIBRARY OF CONGRESS CATALOGING-IN-PUBLICATION DATA

Vowell, Sarah, [date]

Take the cannoli : stories from the New World / Sarah Vowell.

p. cm.

I. Title

AC8 .V76 2000

081—dc21

99-056330

ISBN 0-684-86797-4

FOR GREIL MARCUS AND DAVID RAKOFF

CONTENTS

Take the Cannoli

I love songs about horses, railroads, land, judgment day, family, hard times, whiskey, courtship, marriage, adultery, separation, murder, war, prison, rambling, damnation, home, salvation, death, pride, humor, piety, rebellion, patriotism, larceny, determination, tragedy, rowdiness, heartbreak and love. And Mother. And God.

—JOHNNY CASH

All I wanted was to go somewheres; all I wanted was a change, I warn't particular.

—HUCK FINN ON HELL

HOME MOVIES

Shooting Dad

IF YOU WERE PASSING BY THE HOUSE WHERE I GREW UP DURING MY TEENAGE years and it happened to be before Election Day, you wouldn't have needed to come inside to see that it was a house divided. You could have looked at the Democratic campaign poster in the upstairs window and the Republican one in the downstairs window and seen our home for the Civil War battleground it was. I'm not saying who was the Democrat or who was the Republican—my father or I—but I will tell you that I have never subscribed to *Guns & Ammo*, that I did not plaster the family vehicle with National Rifle Association stickers, and that hunter's orange was never my color.

About the only thing my father and I agree on is the Constitution, though I'm partial to the First Amendment, while he's always favored the Second.

I am a gunsmith's daughter. I like to call my parents' house, located on a quiet residential street in Bozeman, Montana, the United States of Firearms. Guns were everywhere: the so-called pretty ones like the circa 1850 walnut muzzleloader hanging on the wall, Dad's clients' fixer-uppers leaning into corners, an entire rack right next to the TV. I had to move revolvers out of my way to make room for a bowl of Rice Krispies on the kitchen table.

I was eleven when we moved into that Bozeman house. We had never lived in town before, and this was a college town at that. We came from Oklahoma—a dusty little Muskogee County nowhere called Braggs. My parents' property there included an orchard, a horse pasture, and a couple of acres of woods. I knew our lives had changed one morning not long after we moved to Montana when, during breakfast, my father heard a noise and jumped out of his chair. Grabbing a BB gun, he rushed out the front door. Standing in the yard, he started shooting at crows. My mother sprinted after him screaming, "Pat, you might ought to check, but I don't think they do that up here!" From the look on his face, she might as well have told him that his American citizenship had been revoked. He shook his head, mumbling, "Why, shooting crows is a national pastime, like baseball and apple pie." Personally, I preferred baseball and apple pie. I looked up at those crows flying away and thought, I'm going to like it here.

Dad and I started bickering in earnest when I was fourteen, after the 1984 Democratic National Convention. I was so excited when Walter Mondale chose Geraldine Ferraro as his running mate that I taped the front page of the newspaper with her picture on it to the refrigerator door. But there was some sort of mysterious gravity surge in the kitchen. Somehow, that picture ended up in the trash all the way across the room.

Nowadays, I giggle when Dad calls me on Election Day to cheerfully inform me that he has once again canceled out my vote, but I was not always so mature. There were times when I found the fact that he was a gunsmith horrifying. And just *weird*. All he ever cared about were guns. All I ever cared about was art. There were years and years when he hid out by himself in the garage making rifle barrels and I holed up in my room reading Allen Ginsberg poems, and we were incapable of having a conversation that didn't end in an argument.

Our house was partitioned off into territories. While the kitchen and the living room were well within the DMZ, the respective work spaces governed by my father and me were jealously guarded totalitarian states in which each of us declared ourselves dictator. Dad's shop was a messy disaster area, a labyrinth of lathes. Its walls were hung with the mounted antlers of deer he'd bagged, forming a makeshift museum of death. The available flat surfaces were buried under a million scraps of paper on which he sketched his mechanical inventions in blue ball-point pen. And the floor, carpeted with spiky metal shavings, was a tetanus shot waiting to happen. My domain was the cramped, cold space known as the music room. It was also a messy disaster area, an obstacle course of musical instruments—piano, trumpet, baritone horn, valve trombone, various percussion doodads (bells!), and recorders. A framed portrait of the French composer Claude Debussy was nailed to the wall. The available flat surfaces were buried under piles of staff paper, on which I penciled in the pompous orchestra music given titles like "Prelude to the Green Door" (named after an O. Henry short story by the way, not the watershed porn flick *Behind the Green Door*) I starting writing in junior high.

It has been my experience that in order to impress potential suitors, skip the teen Debussy anecdotes and stick with the always attention-getting line "My dad makes guns." Though it won't cause the guy to like me any better, it will make him handle the inevitable breakup with diplomacy—just in case I happen to have any loaded family heirlooms lying around the house.

But the fact is, I have only shot a gun once and once was plenty. My twin sister, Amy, and I were six years old—six—when Dad decided that it was high time we learned how to shoot. Amy remembers the day he handed us the gun for the first time differently. She liked it.

Amy shared our father's enthusiasm for firearms and the quick-draw cowboy mythology surrounding them. I tended to daydream through Dad's activities—the car trip to Dodge City's Boot Hill, his beloved John Wayne Westerns on TV. My sister, on the other hand, turned into Rooster Cogburn Jr., devouring Duke movies with Dad. In fact, she named her teddy bear Duke, hung a colossal John Wayne portrait next to her bed, and took to wearing one of those John Wayne shirts that button on the side. So when Dad led us out to the backyard when we were six and, to Amy's delight, put the gun in her hand, she says she felt it meant that Daddy trusted us and that he thought of us as "big girls."

But I remember holding the pistol only made me feel small. It was so heavy in my hand. I stretched out my arm and pointed it away and winced. It was a very long time before I had the nerve to pull the trigger and I was so scared I had to close my eyes. It felt like it just went off by itself, as if I had no say in the matter, as if the gun just had this *need*. The sound it made was as big as God. It kicked little me back to the ground like a bully, like a foe. It hurt. I don't know if I dropped it or just handed it back over to my dad, but I do know that I never wanted to touch another one again. And, because I believed in the devil, I did what my mother told me to do every time I felt an evil presence. I looked at the smoke and whispered under my breath, "Satan, I rebuke thee."

It's not like I'm saying I was traumatized. It's more like I was decided. Guns: Not For Me. Luckily, both my parents grew up in exasperating households where children were considered puppets and/or slaves. My mom and dad were hell-bent on letting my sister and me make our own choices. So if I decided that I didn't want my father's little death sticks to kick me to the ground again, that was fine with him. He would go hunting with my sister, who started calling herself "the loneliest twin in history" because of my reluctance to engage in family activities.

Of course, the fact that I was allowed to voice my opinions did not mean that my father would silence his own. Some things were said during the Reagan administration that cannot be taken back. Let's just say that I blamed Dad for nuclear proliferation and Contra aid. He believed that if I had my way, all the guns would be confiscated and it would take the commies about fifteen minutes to parachute in and assume control.

We're older now, my dad and I. The older I get, the more I'm interested in becoming a better daughter. First on my list: Figure out the whole gun thing.

Not long ago, my dad finished his most elaborate tool of death yet. A cannon. He built a nineteenth-century cannon. From scratch. It took two years.

My father's cannon is a smaller replica of a cannon called the Big Horn Gun in front of Bozeman's Pioneer Museum. The barrel of the original has been filled with concrete ever since some high school kids in the '50s pointed it at the school across the street and shot out its windows one night as a prank. According to Dad's historical source, a man known to scholars as A Guy at the Museum, the cannon was brought to Bozeman around 1870, and was used by local white merchants to fire at the Sioux and Cheyenne Indians who blocked their trade access to the East in 1874.

"Bozeman was founded on greed," Dad says. The courthouse cannon, he continues, "definitely killed Indians. The merchants filled it full of nuts, bolts, and chopped-up horseshoes. Sitting Bull could have been part of these engagements. They definitely ticked off the Indians, because a couple of years later, Custer wanders into them at Little Bighorn. The Bozeman merchants were out to cause trouble. They left fresh baked bread with cyanide in it on the trail to poison a few Indians."

Because my father's sarcastic American history yarns rarely go on for long before he trots out some nefarious ancestor of ours—I come from a long line of moonshiners, Confederate soldiers, murderers, even Democrats—he cracks that the merchants hired some "community-minded Southern soldiers from North Texas." These soldiers had, like my great-great-grandfather John Vowell, fought under pro-slavery guerrilla William C. Quantrill. Quantrill is most famous for riding into Lawrence, Kansas, in 1863 flying a black flag and commanding his men pharaohlike to "kill every male and burn down every house."

"John Vowell," Dad says, "had a little rep for killing people." And since he abandoned my great-grandfather Charles, whose mother died giving birth to him in 1870, and wasn't seen again until 1912, Dad doesn't rule out the possibility that John Vowell could have been one of the hired guns on the Bozeman Trail. So the cannon isn't just another gun to my dad. It's a map of all his obsessions—firearms, certainly, but also American history and family history, subjects he's never bothered separating from each other.

After tooling a million guns, after inventing and building a rifle barrel boring machine, after setting up that complicated shop filled with lathes and blueing tanks and outmoded blacksmithing tools, the cannon is his most ambitious project ever. I thought that if I was ever going to understand the ballistic bee in his bonnet, this was my chance. It was the biggest gun he ever made and I could experience it and spend time with it with the added bonus of not having to actually pull a trigger myself.

I called Dad and said that I wanted to come to Montana and watch him shoot off the cannon. He was immediately suspicious. But I had never taken much interest in his work before and he would take what he could get. He loaded the cannon into the back of his truck and we drove up into the Bridger Mountains. I was a little worried that the National Forest Service would object to us lobbing fiery balls of metal onto its property. Dad laughed, assuring me that "you cannot shoot fireworks, but this is considered a fire*arm*."

It is a small cannon, about as long as a baseball bat and as wide as a coffee can. But it's heavy—110 pounds. We park near the side of the hill. Dad takes his gunpowder and other tools out of this adorable wooden box on which he has stenciled "PAT G. VOWELL CANNON-WORKS." Cannonworks: So that's what NRA members call a metal-strewn garage.

Dad plunges his homemade bullets into the barrel, points it at an embankment just to be safe, and lights the fuse. When the fuse is lit, it resembles a cartoon. So does the sound, which warrants Ben Day dot words along the lines of *ker-pow!* There's so much Fourth of July smoke everywhere I feel compelled to sing the national anthem.

I've given this a lot of thought—how to convey the giddiness I felt when the cannon shot off. But there isn't a sophisticated way to say this. It's just really, really cool. My dad thought so, too.

Sometimes, I put together stories about the more eccentric corners of the American experience for public radio. So I happen to have my tape recorder with me, and I've never seen levels like these. Every time the cannon goes off, the delicate needles which keep track of the sound quality lurch into the bad, red zone so fast and so hard I'm surprised they don't break.

The cannon was so loud and so painful, I had to touch my head to make sure my skull hadn't cracked open. One thing that my dad and I share is that we're both a little hard of hearing—me from Aerosmith, him from gunsmith.

He lights the fuse again. The bullet knocks over the log he was aiming at. I instantly utter a sentence I never in my entire life thought I would say. I tell him, "Good shot, Dad."

Just as I'm wondering what's coming over me, two hikers walk by. Apparently, they have never seen a man set off a homemade cannon in the middle of the wilderness while his daughter holds a foot-long microphone up into the air recording its terrorist boom. One hiker gives me a puzzled look and asks, "So you work for the radio and that's your dad?"

Dad shoots the cannon again so that they can see how it works. The other hiker says, "That's quite the machine you got there." But he isn't talking about the cannon. He's talking about my tape recorder and my microphone—which is called a *shotgun* mike. I stare back at him, then I look over at my father's cannon, then down at my microphone, and I think, Oh. My. God. My dad and I are the same person. We're both smart-alecky loners with goofy projects and weird equipment. And since this whole target practice outing was my idea, I was no longer his adversary. I was his accomplice. What's worse, I was liking it.

I haven't changed my mind about guns. I can get behind the cannon because it is a completely ceremonial object. It's unwieldy and impractical, just like everything else I care about. Try to rob a convenience store with this 110-pound Saturday night special, you'd still be dragging it in the door Sunday afternoon.

I love noise. As a music fan, I'm always waiting for that moment in a song when something just flies out of it and explodes in the air. My dad is a one-man garage band, the kind of rock 'n' roller who slaves away at his art for no reason other than to make his own sound. My dad is an artist—a pretty driven, idiosyncratic one, too. He's got his last *Gesamtkunstwerk* all planned out. It's a performance piece. We're all in it—my mom, the loneliest twin in history, and me.

When my father dies, take a wild guess what he wants done with his ashes. Here's a hint: It requires a cannon.

"You guys are going to love this," he smirks, eyeballing the cannon. "You get to drag this thing up on top of the Gravellies on opening day of hunting season. And looking off at Sphinx Mountain, you get to put me in little paper bags. I can take my last hunting trip on opening morning."

I'll do it, too. I will have my father's body burned into ashes. I will pack these ashes into paper bags. I will go to the mountains with my mother, my sister, and the cannon. I will plunge his remains into the barrel and point it into a hill so that he doesn't take anyone with him. I will light the fuse. But I will not cover my ears. Because when I blow what used to be my dad into the earth, I want it to hurt.

Music Lessons

IT WAS AUTUMN IN AMERICA, A FINE HOT INDIAN SUMMER DAY. PRETTY HIGH school girls sat on bleachers with the sun shining in their pretty hair, watching handsome high school boys play footfall. And then, it was halftime, which is where I came in.

I was standing in line in my silver spats down past the end zone waiting to go on. I was in marching band. I had a foot-tall, fake fur black hat, with the vaguely processed food name "shako," strapped under my chin. The shako's purpose is to make a scrubby assortment of adolescents look magisterial. But it not only prevented me from breathing, it rendered me and my comrades in the horn section unstable, so that even though my job was to march around as some kind of sick metaphor for teenage military precision, I moved through time and space with the grace and confidence of a puppy walking on a beach ball.

Because of my double shortage of strength and coordination, I barely passed gym. But somehow, I was supposed to lift a baritone horn that measured twice my body weight, blow into it while reading microscopic sheet music, step in a straight line while remembering left foot on beats one and three, right foot on beats two and four, and maneuver myself into cute visual formations, like the trio of stick figures we fashioned when we played the theme from *My Three Sons*.

Halfway through the halftime program, I had to break formation, drop my baritone horn on the field, and sprint to the fifty-yard line—a long haul—with everyone in the band, the pretty girls in the bleachers, and the football players on the sidelines all watching and waiting, silent and still. At midfield I picked up my mallets and—this is what they had been waiting for—I pounded out a xylophone solo on a little Latin-flavored number called "Tico Tico."

My polo shirt—clad nemesis Andy Heap stood up in the stands screaming, "Vowell! Vowell! Whooooo! Whoooo!", as the laughter of his friends, at me, drowned out the horn section. This was the same Andy Heap, I might add, who earlier in the week in music history class had delivered an oral report on Tchaikovsky's lady friend, calling her Mimi throughout (even though her name was Nadya). Andy Heap was apparently smart enough to publicly humiliate me during "Tico Tico," he just wasn't smart enough to know that the abbreviation "Mme." stands not for Mimi, but "Madame."

I only had a second to stick out my tongue at Andy when I finished "Tico Tico," because I had to let go of the mallets, rush over to my baritone—again, the freeze-framed spectators, the loneliness of the long-distance runner—and I'm back in formation with the low brass for the finale.

I was getting academic credit for this, to wear that uniform to play those songs. I was getting graded. Which begs the question: What exactly was I supposed to be learning? What was marching band supposed to teach me? Because marching isn't a particularly applicable skill in later life. Here then, some lessons—actually useful ones—I accidentally learned while pursuing music.

ACCIDENTAL LESSON #1: MARXISM FOR TENTH GRADERS

Once a week, the best band kids played with the orchestra. I played the bass drum in orchestra, which meant that I never got to play. My participation ratio was something like seventy-five measures of rest per one big bass wallop. This gave me plenty of time to contemplate the class warfare of the situation. Here's what I figured out: Orchestra kids wear tuxedos. Band kids wear tuxedo T-shirts.

The orchestra kids, with their brown woolens and Teutonic last names, had the well-scrubbed, dark blond aura of a Hitler Youth brigade. These were the sons and daughters of humanities professors. They took German. They played soccer. Dumping the fluorescent T-shirts of the band kids into the orchestra each week must have looked like tossing a handful of Skittles into a box of Swiss chocolates.

But nothing brings kids together like hate. The one thing the band kids and the orchestra kids had in common was a unified disgust for the chorus kids, who were, to us, merely drama geeks with access to four-part harmony. A shy violin player wasn't likely to haunt the halls between classes playing *Eine Kleine Nachtmusik* any more than a band kid would blare "Land of 1000 Dances" on his tuba more than three inches outside the band room door. But that didn't stop the choir girls from making everyone temporarily forget their locker combinations thanks to an impromptu, uncalled-for burst from *Brigadoon*.

Andy Heap: chorus.

ACCIDENTAL LESSON #2: WHERE'S WALTER?

My junior high had an electronic music lab. We made tape loops and learned words like "quadraphonic." In my spare time, just for fun, I checked out all the books on electronic music from the library. My favorite records for a while there were Walter Carlos's concept albums *Switched-On Bach* and its sequel, *The Well-Tempered Synthesizer*, which offered what I thought were hilariously witty covers of Bach classics performed on (get this) a Moog synthesizer. What kind of madcap visionary was capable of turning eighteenth-century fugues into machine-age mongrels?

In my readings on electronic music, something puzzled me. Every time I'd look into Walter Carlos, the information would just stop and someone named Wendy Carlos would turn up. I got to school early one morning to ask my electronic-music teacher what happened to Walter and was Wendy Walter's wife or daughter? He didn't answer for a long time. Then he blurted out, "Uh, Wendy *is* Walter."

What did he mean?

"Walter had a sex change operation and changed his name to Wendy."

What's a sex change operation? I had just started eighth grade. I knew absolutely nothing about sex. We didn't talk about it in my family and sex ed wasn't scheduled until spring. I was a wholesome, small-town Christian kid engaged in what I thought were wholesome, small-town Christian pursuits. It's Bach for heaven's sake. Suddenly, bam, I'm standing at the corner of Sodom and Gomorrah and where's my street map?

That Walter Carlos. I hadn't even recovered from the shock that Bach could be messed with.

ACCIDENTAL LESSON #3:
BIOLOGY AS DESTINY

In seventh grade, I started band. I wanted to play the drums. My parents, who lived with me—as was the custom in Montana—did not want me to play the drums. So I picked the next loudest instrument instead—the trumpet. How I loved my trumpet, the feel of it in my hands, its very volume and shine. I especially loved the illicitly named spit valve.

In eighth grade, a teacher told me about this good old trumpet player I might like so I went out and bought one of his records. And every night, for over a year, I went to sleep listening to it, the same songs over and over, trying to figure out why Louis Armstrong was so moving, so funny, so good. I got caught up in this superstar talent of his right around the time I was beginning to suspect that I didn't have it, talent that is.

There was another problem which I discovered about three years into my trumpet career. I found out that the reason I had shoddy tone and trouble hitting the high notes was because of the shape of my jaw. I felt my life was more or less over. I was outraged that a person's fate could depend on something as arbitrary as the angles of her teeth. And not only that, I had to switch to a brass instrument with a bigger mouthpiece—the baritone horn. The baritone horn. Like, trumpets are played by Miles Davis and baritones are played by *nobody*.

ACCIDENTAL LESSON #4:
HE'S SCHROEDER, I'M CHARLIE BROWN

One of the reasons I knew I wasn't God's gift to music was that I went to school with him—the living, breathing personification of entertainment—Jon Wilson. Jon Wilson could play the piano. Like REALLY. PLAY. THE PIANO. He knew all the crowd-pleasing keyboard favorites. Kids would come up to him and request the Charlie Brown theme song or Van Halen's "Jump" so often I'm surprised he didn't roll a baby grand with an empty milk carton on top into the junior high cafeteria and play for tips during lunch.

The thing that bothered me about Jon Wilson, who was actually a pretty nice guy, was that people loved him! Loved him! And our friendly competition heated up when we both got serious about writing music. By fifteen, I was composing orchestral scores which went unperformed for the most part, and justifiably so. They were difficult, unlistenable, and wildly pretentious, though, thankfully, I didn't learn the word "pretentious" until I was eighteen, thereby freeing me up to be unbearably guilt-free for most of my adolescence. My compositions were informed by the repetitive minimalist tendencies of Philip Glass. The Glass method, which, I read in a magazine, he called "the additive process," involved developing a melody rhythmically. He'd start with two notes within a beat, then up the ante to three, then four, and so on. I loved the idea, and I loved the name. But I also thought, Why wait? Why waste all that time developing an idea over an extended period of time when you could encapsulate the entire concept in one big, loud, twelve-second piece! Why not just have every instrument in an ensemble play every kind of note grouping simultaneously? That way, you could make even the sappiest string section sound almost as good as a hair dryer.

Jon Wilson, on the other hand, wrote sentimental, professional-quality love songs à la Lionel Richie and sang them after school in the band room to his fan base of swooning females. Pishposh, I thought, alone in my two-by-three soundproof practice module that was more than roomy enough to accommodate my admirers. I was convinced that real artists were the kind that nobody understood, much less liked, which was pretty reassuring since nobody liked me. Or my music.

ACCIDENTAL LESSON #5: WHEN DOVES CRY

From the time I was twelve until I finished high school at eighteen, my poor parents' calendar was blackened by an ambitious roster of concerts and recitals averaging at least one per month. They were always so gushy in their support, it never occurred to me that they might have preferred to avoid junior high school gymnasium performances of the theme from *Rocky*. They acted as though their world revolved around my sister and me, so that's what we believed.

I remember one night, after an eighth-grade band concert, I caught a glimpse of pencil marks on my father's rolled-up program. He told me that he checked off each movement of each piece as it ended. Obviously because he was counting the seconds until he could go home. At the time, I took it badly. I was offended that he had so little regard for the seriousness of our thoughtful, well-rehearsed interpretation of "What Do You Do with a Drunken Sailor." Now, I see those pathetic little checkmarks as heart-shaped symbols of his love.

Everyone says that love requires the utmost honesty, but that's not entirely true. Once I knew that my father was suffering for my sake—really suffering—I learned that love, especially the parental kind, requires the heartwarming sacrifice that can only accompany fake enthusiasm.

ACCIDENTAL LESSON #6:
BIRTH OF THE COOL

So: I was doomed at the trumpet. I was also acceptable at the baritone, shaky on the xylophone, and putrid on the piano. But there was one instrument for which I had an innate knack, an instrument I could play with some semblance of grace. It was, unfortunately, an instrument already on its way out of fashion during the lifetime of J. S. Bach: the recorder. I taught myself to play it, and by fourteen, I was perhaps the youngest member of the American Recorder Society, reading their journal, *American Recorder*, and practicing the Elizabethan and baroque music I special-ordered with my baby-sitting money.

I found out about an amateur ensemble that met once a week in my town, playing mostly Elizabethan standards like "It Was a Lover and His Lass" at a tempo marked on the metronome as *Post Office Slow*. The members of the Bozeman Recorder Ensemble, as we were called, included a retired high school music teacher, two Montana State University math professors, and a number of housewives, one of whom had a daughter in my grade. I was the only member under the age of forty and most of them would have been eligible for the senior citizen discount at the music store. I played with them for a couple of years, until my pals Margaret and Leota—the wives of the dean of the College of Arts and Architecture and a physics professor respectively—and I broke off to form our own trio. The three of us just liked each other, liked playing. At school, in all those actual hours of actual classes with actual teachers, music felt more like a job. Playing with Leota and Margaret was the first time—the only time—I actually enjoyed playing music.

We played gigs, too, at the library, at street fairs. Imagine playing an Elizabethan ballad such as my favorite, a sad wail called "Willow Willow," on the street with your two friends who happen to be older than your parents. You might look up from your music stand and notice one of your schoolmates staring on in horror. Andy Heap, for instance. But you know what? You don't care. You might even smile at him. And this is the most important lesson of marching band, of public displays of recorder. To withstand embarrassment. Maybe even seek it out. To take nerdiness to its most dizzying "Willow Willow," "Tico Tico" extremes, and stand before my peers with my head held high. To stick out my tongue at the Andy Heaps of the world, run back to the baritone horn of life, and blow mighty and proud.

The End Is Near,
Nearer, Nearest

WHEN THE PLANE IS GOING DOWN, YOU SUDDENLY FEEL THE URGE TO HUG that smelly, snoring person in the seat next to you. Because nothing brings people together like doom. And I should know. I've been to more potlucks, picnics, and get-togethers organized around the idea that we're all going to die than I care to count. Not that I'm trivializing the Apocalypse; I'm sure the actual end of the world will involve a lot of wailing and gnashing of teeth. But in my experience, talking about the end of the world is a proven way to make friends.

APOCALYPSE 1: MARK OF THE BEAST

I've had this recurring dream since I was six years old: My mother's gone. She is not running-errands gone, not at-a-friend's-house gone. She's gone for good, vanished. My sister's still here. My dad's around. In fact, all the kids and dads in town are present and accounted for but all the mothers have vanished overnight. That's how I figure out the rapture's happened. Only the women are worthy enough of God's grace to get whisked off to heaven. The wicked men and wicked children are left to tough out Armageddon on our own.

That means my sister and I will have to suffer through the lake of fire, the rivers of blood, and our father's cooking. Once I get sick of puking up his specialties—spaghetti sandwiches and a greasy tinfoil concoction he liked to call Boy Scout potatoes—I go to the supermarket, Gibson's in Muskogee. I fill a cart with food. At the checkout counter, I line up vegetables on the conveyor belt by the cash register. The clerk informs me that in order to pay for the food, I must take the mark of the beast. She stands ready to attach a "666" price tag to my forehead. I refuse. Soldiers with machine guns appear. They gun me down, my blood spattering all over the salad fixin's. Then, poof, I'm in heaven, dead, harp in hand.

I still have that dream sometimes. And thinking about it now, as an atheistic adult, I realize how many things are going on in it, that it is a microcosm of my childhood world. At my Oklahoma church, Braggs Pentecostal Holiness, the sermons were about the Book of Revelation when I was in first grade—the year I learned to read. So Revelation, the Bible's final chapter and the one that chronicles the end of the world, was the first book of the Bible I ever read myself. That loophole about not accepting the mark of the beast being a viable way for rapture-missers to get into heaven comes from Scripture, as does the grocery store setting. According to Revelation 13:17: "And that no man might buy or sell, save he that had the mark, or the name of the beast, or the number of his name." And that number, of course, revealed in verse 18, is "six hundred threescore and six": 666. The other reason I refuse the mark in the grocery store is tied up in the fundamentalist uproar over bar codes in the 1970s; bar codes were thought by many to be the mark of the beast.

I was a believer. But there was something stronger than my belief in God. The thing the preacher said that I believed more than anything else I heard at church was that I was a sinner. When I sang "Amazing Grace," the key phrase wasn't the title's promise of redemption but this: *wretch like me*. Even as a six-year-old I knew I'd never be good enough to get into heaven. Thus I seized on the escape clause I dreamed about, the idea that I could refuse the mark of the beast at a grocery store and everything would be all right. I knew I was evil, I knew I couldn't get through a lifetime adhering to daily virtue, but I was pretty sure I had the guts to withstand two or three seconds of machine-gun pain when the time came. This comforted me. It kept me from panicking about the eternal consequences of every childish trespass.

Still, Armageddon is kind of a lot to lay on a six-year-old. The Book of Revelation includes verse after verse of dragons and demons and the blood of the lamb. A typical passage reads, "And the fourth angel poured out his vial upon the sun; and power was given unto him to scorch men with fire." Frankly, I could have done with fewer seven seals and more seven dwarves.

There are people in this country who will argue that because of the demise of morals in general and Sunday school in particular kids today are losing their innocence before they should, that because of cartoons and Ken Starr and curricula about their classmates who have two mommies, youth learn too much too soon about sex and death. Well, like practically everyone else in the Western world who came of age since Gutenberg, I lost my innocence the old-time-religion way, by reading the nursery rhyme of fornication that is the Old Testament and the fairy tale of bloodbath that is the New. Job taught me Hey! Life's not fair! Lot's wife taught me that I'm probably going to come across a few weird sleazy things I won't be able to resist looking into. And the Book of Revelation taught me to live in the moment, if only because the future's so grim.

Being a fundamentalist means going straight to the source. I was asked to not only read the Bible, but to memorize Bible verses. If it wasn't for the easy access to the sordid Word of God I might have had an innocent childhood. Instead, I was a worrywart before my time, shivering in constant fear of a god who, from what I could tell, huffed and puffed around the cosmos looking like my dad did when my sister refused to take her vitamins that one time.

God wasn't exactly a children's rights advocate. The first thing a child reading the Bible notices is that you're supposed to honor your mother and father but they're not necessarily required to reciprocate. This was a god who told Abraham to knife his boy Isaac and then at the last minute, when the dagger's poised above Isaac's heart, God tells

Abraham that He's just kidding. This was a god who let a child lose his birthright because of some screwball mix-up involving fake fur hands and a bowl of soup. This was a god who saw to it that his own son had his hands and feet nailed onto pieces of wood.

God, for me, was not in the details. I still set store by the big Judeo-Christian messages. Who can argue with the Ten Commandments? Don't kill anybody; don't mess around with other people's spouses; be nice to your mom and dad. Fine advice. It was the minutiae that nagged at me.

One of my favorite television characters was *Star Trek*'s Mr. Spock. I would torment my hotheaded sister, Amy, an extreme child who batted back and forth between only two emotional states—love and hate—by reproaching her feverish fits (while ducking her punches) with the comeback "You are being *so* irrational." Same goes for church. My Spockish nature tended to clash with some of the more fanciful details of Bible theory and practice that are part of Pentecostal life.

It was made clear to me that I wasn't supposed to trouble the moody Creator with any pesky questions about the eccentricities of His cosmic system. So when I asked about stuff that confused me, like "How come we're praying for the bar to be shut down when Jesus himself turned water into wine?", I was shushed and told to have faith. Thus my idea of heaven was that I got to spend eternity sitting at the feet of God, grilling Him. "Let me get this straight," I'd say by way of introduction. "It's your position that every person ever born has to suffer because Eve couldn't resist a healthy between-meals snack?" Once I got the metaphysical queries out of the way I could satisfy my curiosity about how He came up with stuff I was learning about in school, like photosynthesis.

Until the mark-of-the-beast police machine-gunned me to that Great Q & A in the Sky, I soon figured out that I should keep my qualms to myself. Christianity is no different from any other cult—it isn't about faith. It's *about* agreement, about like-minded people sitting together in the same room at the same time believing the same thing. That unity is its appeal. Once someone, even a little six-year-old someone wearing patent leather Mary Janes, starts asking questions that can't be answered, the whole congregation's fun is spoiled. (Though my mouth was the least of my mother's worries at church. My sister's constant childish fidgeting was a more pressing concern. During one Sunday sermon, as Mom was dragging the little hellion out to the parking lot for a spanking, Amy kicked at the pews screaming at the congregation, "Pray for me!")

However much I privately questioned the logic of Genesis, I never once doubted the inevitability of Revelation, never once doubted that the world would end. Because living in eastern Oklahoma and believing in the Apocalypse made a lot of sense. When I read the part in Revelation about the Four Horsemen of the Apocalypse, how the end times will be set in motion by horses breathing fire and brimstone, it reminded me of the near-death trips I'd taken with my own pet, Stockings. My dad had given me a Tennessee walking horse—but not a saddle. And so I rode bareback, clutching Stockings's mane, praying that she wouldn't get spooked, though she always did, tearing off into the woods, breathing fire. By the time she stopped, after thirty-nine thousand repetitions of the command "Whoa!", the hickory branches would have etched my skin into a bloody gingham. If one of the four horses of the Apocalypse had to be put down, Stockings was ready to ride.

I could buy the gaudy deaths and grisly details set forth in Revelation because Oklahoma itself was a biblical landscape. We must have been on tornado watch half the year. And the place was literally crawling with snakes—snakes in my treehouse, snakes on the porch, snakes in the yard, snakes on Rainbow Mountain, which my mom found out the hard way used to be named Snake Mountain after one of its copperheads put her in the hospital. Because I was baptized when I was eight in a water moccasin–infested lake, and, as if I wasn't petrified enough (fangs and drowning being two of my bigger fears), Sister Minnie's drunken husband drove up to the water's edge in his pickup right after I came up for air and he started scream-singing the hymn "Shall We Gather at the River." Because our cousin Gary John's wife got shot dead in the head with Gary's own gun by Gary's sister's husband, who was joking around and didn't know the gun was loaded, ha-ha. Because the leader of my Brownie troop was smashed into a million pieces trying to cross the train tracks. Because my grandfather Pa Vowell buried another wife every few years. Because my other grandfather Pa Parson was a Cherokee wart doctor who could tie a string around a wart and bury the string in the ground and that made the wart go away. Because my grandmother Ma Parson lost her mind one day and couldn't remember my name though she could remember all the words to "Bringing In the Sheaves" and today we call this Alzheimer's but back then we called it "God's will." Because on Wednesday nights my mother would drive this ancient witchy widow to church—a lady who believed haircuts for women were a sin, which did stop her from trimming that mangy white rope dangling off her scalp around 1923 but did not stop her from scamming rides off my mom (a former hairdresser); my sister and I dreaded the moment the woman climbed into the car because she'd give us the evil eye and tell us that our perky, little-girl pixie cuts were some kind of fatal flaw we'd go to hell for.

So in such a superstitious town among such accident-prone citizens, Revelation seemed more like a gossip sheet than a ghost story. In fact, considering all the random wrath of God around me, Armageddon appeared refreshingly well thought-out. And that was its attraction to everyone at church. We gathered together to reassure one another that no matter what horrible thing just happened, no matter whose daughter just got scraped off the train tracks, whose mother was in the hospital with fang marks perforating her leg, God had a plan. A cruel, kooky, murderous horror movie of a plan for sure, but a plan nonetheless.

That's what even the gloomiest sermons were about—the future. And that's why in the gospel hymns we sang, "will" was the most popular verb—"I will meet you in the morning," "There will be peace in the valley someday," and my favorite, "I'll fly away." Even now, a quarter of a century after I learned those songs, they're still stuck in my head. I miss singing them. I miss the harmony. Some Sunday mornings, in the middle of secular superstitious rituals like reading *The New York Times Magazine* or watching that berserk Sam Donaldson on TV, I'll hum "I'll fly away" as I make coffee, remembering what it was like to have a Sunday morning purpose, remembering what it was like to have someplace to go, even if it was just hell.

APOCALYPSE 2:
THIS COULD HAPPEN TO YOU

I'm not exactly proud to admit this, but I owe my life to Ronald Reagan. My family moved from Oklahoma to Montana in 1981, the year Reagan was inaugurated. I was eleven. Away from the Bible Belt, my family was forced to attend a bland, nondenominational church about which my mother said, "Too much teachin', not enough preachin'." Religion became an increasingly less urgent part of my life.

This did not mean that the end of the world faded from the forefront of my psyche. I merely replaced one apocalypse for another. In the early '80s, President Reagan made so many mortifying announcements about the "evil empire" and his Strategic Defense Initiative, a.k.a. Star Wars, and "We begin bombing in five minutes" jokes that I was utterly convinced I was not going to grow up. By 1983, he'd made the whole country so nervous that there was a prime-time TV movie about nuclear winter called *The Day After*. I have never seen the movie, however, because my mother decided our family wouldn't be watching it as that would be "too disturbing." I guess talking to six-year-olds about the reign of the Antichrist is fine, but letting teenagers watch Jason Robards stumble through rubble for a couple of hours on TV is unthinkable.

What with waking up every morning surprised there was still a world to wake up to, I was not a particularly fun-loving high school student. By junior year—1986, Chernobyl—my free time was filled up with doing my homework and writing orchestra music derivative of my then-hero, Philip Glass, repetitive music predicated on the notion that time, perhaps, is going nowhere. Ah, sweet sixteen. But then my more sociable sister, Amy, told me that some kids she knew from art class were starting an antinuclear group. I was immediately excited, impressed.

I only knew the kids who, like me, took band. I thought the art class students who showed up for the first meeting of what would become Youth for Global Peace were the most glamorous people I'd ever met. They played in rock 'n' roll bands and wrote poetry and didn't eat meat. They had spiky hair and smoked cigarettes and debated whether or not William Burroughs's *Junky* was better than his *Naked Lunch*.

Yeah, yeah, we talked about nukes. We were . . . against them. We'd meet every Saturday night at Greta Montagne's house and oftentimes some adult from the local chapter of Alliance for a Nuclear Free Future would talk about some nuclear subject. We made antinuke T-shirts and wore them to school. We handed out pie charts of Reagan's 1986 federal budget (in which defense spending was the biggest slice of pie) at grocery store parking lots. We got up really early one morning and plastered the school walls with xeroxed posters of a mushroom cloud on which we scribbled "This Could Happen to You." We had a No Nukes banner in the homecoming parade (which I couldn't walk behind because I was up front playing baritone horn in the marching band). My biggest contribution was probably representing the group in a roundtable discussion on the local public television channel; the adults said a few mundane things about a saner nuclear policy before I started screaming, "You got to grow up! Do you know what it's like to think you're not going to grow up? Do you?" Why the station manager didn't immediately grasp my broadcasting potential then and there based on my nuanced, articulate approach and offer me my own show remains a mystery.

In retrospect the antinuclear part of the antinuclear group was the least important thing for me. For starters, they introduced me to the Beat Generation. I remember the first time I read Allen Ginsberg's poem "America," with its famous line that America should "Go fuck yourself with your atom bomb." I didn't know you could say that in a poem, but I recognized the sentiment. Later in the poem Ginsberg writes, "It occurs to me that I am America." I loved that line because it solved a problem, because it shook its queer fist at the rest of the words, words about being a stranger in a strange land. I was more alienated than usual that year. Eleventh grade is the year Montana students are required to take American history and American literature. I was having trouble matching up the founding fathers' ideals we read about in history class and the less mythic goings-on in Reagan's Washington I read about in the newspaper. I was having trouble matching up Ralph Waldo Emerson's essay "Self-Reliance" and the cookie-cutter mandate of high school social customs. (Though I did relish the moment in English class when I was asked to read "Self-Reliance" aloud. I got to look the boy who always called me "weirdo" in the eye and proclaim, "Whoso would be a *man*, must be a nonconformist." My italics.) I admired Emerson's lone-wolf laments, but I needed the Beats more.

The Beats wrote about a freewheeling alternative to the rigid social confines of the 1950s. I have only a vague, secondhand notion of what it must have been like to be young and uneasy and outraged in the Eisenhower era. But I have an intimate knowledge of what it was like to be young and uneasy and outraged under Reagan. My high school was 1980s America in miniature—you either belonged or you didn't. And if you didn't, you learned to seek relief where you could find it—and for me, that relief was with the other black-clad malcontents who could quote defense-spending statistics even though we were barely passing algebra. The people in the antinuke group weren't just my friends, they were my congregation, and our bible was Kerouac's *On the Road*. Even though we spent our days watching clocks crawl, that book taught us that there was fast music and fast thinking ahead, that there were jazzy, drunken highways leading out of purgatory, to the West Coast, to the East Coast, anywhere but there.

Except that, deep down, I didn't believe I'd live long enough to hear that music, to get out of town. I thought I'd be blown to bits, probably sitting in Mr. Crowley's French class, conjugating verbs in the future tense at the precise moment my future went up in smoke. But I wanted more than anything to do what Kerouac did, to conjugate American verbs and write pretty sentences that stretched on forever, or small, simple ones that said, "Yes, zoom!" I wanted to light out and see the towns of the U.S.A., to notice how the sky looks when the sun goes down over places I'd never been. Elko, Nevada. Flagstaff, Arizona. New Orleans.

That year, a middle-aged acquaintance asked me what my favorite book was and I said, "*On the Road.*" He smiled, said, "That was my favorite book when I was sixteen." At the time, I thought he was patronizing me, that it was going to be my favorite book forever and ever, amen. But he was right. As an adult, I'm more of a *Gatsby* girl—more tragic, more sad, just as interested in what America costs as what it has to offer.

We all grew up, those of us who took *On the Road* to heart. We came to cringe a little at our old favorite poet, concluding that God was likely never Pooh Bear, that sometimes New York and California could be just as isolated as our provincial hometown, and that grown men didn't run back and forth all the time bleeding soup and sympathy out of sucker women. But those are just details, really. We got what we needed, namely a passion for unlikely words, the willingness to improvise, a distrust of authority, and a sentimental attachment to a certain America, still so lovely, as Kerouac wrote, "at lilac evening." I have since played the slots at breakfast in Elko, walked in the Flagstaff moonlight, had the hiccups in New Orleans.

If I'm still wistful about *On the Road,* I look on the rest of the Kerouac oeuvre—the poems, the poems!—in horror. Read *Satori in Paris* lately? But if I had never read Jack Kerouac's horrendous poems, I never would have had the guts to write horrendous poems myself. I never would have signed up for Mrs. Safford's poetry class the spring of junior year, which led me to poetry readings, which introduced me to bad red wine, and after that it's all just one big blurry condemned path to journalism and San Francisco.

As political movements go, our antinuclear group was wildly ineffective. Like, we showed a documentary about the effects of nuclear winter one school lunch period and the only person who showed up to watch it was a West German foreign exchange student. We were much better at getting attention for our other, artier exploits, the most famous of which was a performance-art brouhaha we staged before an unsuspecting English class. We all dressed in black, entering the room one at a time, blankly commanding, "Applause. Applause." (There wasn't any.) Carol Hollier bowed weird whatevers on her cello; I blew into my plastic recorder as hard as I could, pulling it in and out of a bowl of water; Paul Anderson thumped on an African slit drum; Rob Lehrkind recited his poem about how "God is in the drying machine"; and my sister and Nikki Greever flipped a slide projector around to different surrealist artworks, including Méret Oppenheim's 1936 sculpture *Fur-lined Teacup.*

At the time I thought we were, like the Beats and surrealists (and, distant third, nuclear freezers) we so admired, a movement. But now I see that the importance of the group was, for me, that we were friends. I'd had friends before them, but I'd never had a gang, never had a group of people I liked and admired and enjoyed. The antinuke group taught me a lesson which changed my life—how to hang out. For every hour we spent talking about intercontinental ballistic missiles, we spent twelve hours at the 4 B's diner drinking coffee and discussing the glory that was *Eraserhead.* And the first time Matt Brewer, the coolest boy, invited me over to his house and I got there and he and Jimmy Harkin were sitting around listening to Black Sabbath and spray-painting Legos black, I sort of hugged myself—contrary to conventional leftist wisdom—with nuclear arms. I didn't know life could be that fun.

APOCALYPSE 3: AND I FEEL FINE

The Berlin Wall falls. The Cold War ends. I start believing I might live long enough to die of something other than a first-strike Soviet attack or refusing the mark of the beast. Goodbye darkness, my old friend. Remember the good old days? When I was a kid, the end of the world really was something—nuclear holocaust, the rapture. But they don't make apocalypses like they used to. Just look at the cheap little cataclysm they're trying to pass off to unsuspecting futurephobes lately. These kids today and their Y2K: Do they know what it's like to think they're not going to grow up? Do they?

I tried to be interested in Y2K. The newspaper said I should be.

When I was in San Francisco in late 1998, I heard about a community group there which was organizing for the possible Y2K aftermath. And, knowing how the end brings people together, I had to go. But the good people of Bay2K were not the young Silicon Valley computer programmers I'd hoped for. Instead, the group felt very ex-hippie, very New Age, very Marin. One part of the evening ended with a woman chanting a Hopi prayer.

They broke off into small groups to address specific problems, from pragmatic topics like "community preparedness" to—my group—the less tangible "psychological and spiritual issues." One woman says that if nothing's different when she wakes up on the first day of the new millennium, well, at least she had a good excuse to meet her neighbors and "have a really good dialogue."

The dialogue seems to be the point. Just like my old church and my old antinuclear group, they were using the end of the world as a means to meet 'n' greet, planning block parties so they can come up with Y2K contingency plans in their neighborhoods. They talked about how American culture is unsustainable and out of control, stridently opining that we brought this fall on ourselves. (A guy named Rick spun a very witty analogy comparing Silicon Valley to building a house upon the sand.) They were looking forward to a saner, more agrarian way of life. One of the men said neighborhoods should get together and buy a tiller, to start community gardens. To them, Y2K looks a lot like Y1K.

I grew increasingly alarmed at the picture they were painting, a golden picture of neighbor next to neighbor, throwing off the shackles of capitalism to till the soil, at one with the earth. A woman named Leslie said she'd like to help out, but "I'm physically challenged, so I can't even offer my strength. I can't garden. I'd like to but I can't."

The man sitting next to her told her that she could contribute in other ways—like canning. He said, "Even the know-how of doing it is just as valuable as the manpower or the strength to do it."

Each giving according to his abilities, each taking according to his needs: I'm not sure which idea I reacted to more, this brand of shiny happy Marxism—all expressed as if the history of the twentieth century never happened—or the talk about canning. Just picturing mason jars full of stewed tomatoes, a bomb went off inside me. I suddenly realized what they were proposing—canning, gardening, spending time with your neighbors. This is Oklahoma, minus God, the one thing that gave it all some dignity.

Maybe my problem with working up interest in Y2K was that I suffer from apocalypse fatigue. I've outgrown Armageddon. I don't need the end of the world to make friends anymore. Though far be it from me to begrudge anyone his own millennial vision, whatever apocalyptic scenario gives him a reason to leave the house, slap on a name tag, and have a really good dialogue.

While I'm hardly the most optimistic American, I did not share the Y2K group's wholly cynical picture of current events. Heaven, such as it is, is right here on earth. Behold: my revelation: I stand at the door in the morning, and lo, there is a newspaper, in sight like unto an emerald. And holy, holy, holy is the coffee, which was, and is, and is to come. And hark, I hear the voice of an angel round about the radio, saying, "Since my baby left me I found a new place to dwell." And lo, after this I beheld a great multitude, which no man could number, of shoes. And after these things I will hasten unto a taxicab and to a theater, where a ticket will be given unto me, and lo, it will be a matinee, and a film that doeth great wonders. And when it is finished, the heavens will open, and out will cometh a rain fragrant as myrrh, and yea, I have an umbrella.

POST CARDS

Take the Cannoli

THERE COMES A TIME HALFWAY THROUGH ANY HALFWAY DECENT LIBERAL arts major's college career when she no longer has any idea what she believes. She flies violently through air polluted by conflicting ideas and theories, never stopping at one system of thought long enough to feel at home. All those books, all that talk, and, oh, the self-reflection. Am I an existentialist? A Taoist? A transcendentalist? A modernist, a postmodernist? A relativist-positivist-historicist-dadaist-deconstructionist? Was I Apollonian? Was I Dionysian (or just drunk)? Which was right and which was wrong, *impressionism* or *expressionism*? And while we're at it, is there such a thing as right and wrong?

Until I figured out that the flight between questions is itself a workable system, I craved answers, rules. A code. So by my junior year, I was spending part of every week, sometimes every day, watching *The Godfather* on videotape.

The Godfather was an addiction. And like all self-respecting addicts, I did not want anyone to find out about my habit. Which was difficult considering that I shared a house with my boyfriend and two other roommates, all of whom probably thought my profound interest in their class schedules had to do with love and friendship. But I needed to know when the house would be empty so I could watch snippets of the film. Sometimes it took weeks to get through the whole thing. If I had a free hour between earth science lab and my work-study job, I'd sneak home and get through the scene where Sonny Corleone is gunned down at the toll booth, his shirt polka-dotted with bullet holes. Or, if I finished writing a paper analyzing American mediocrity according to Alexis de Tocqueville, I'd reward myself with a few minutes of Michael Corleone doing an excellent job of firing a pistol into a police captain's face. But if the phone rang while I was watching, I turned off the sound so that the caller wouldn't guess what I was up to. I thought that if anyone knew how much time I was spending with the Corleones, they would think it was some desperate cry for help. I always pictured the moment I was found out as a scene from a movie, a movie considerably less epic than *The Godfather*: My concerned boyfriend would eject the tape from the VCR with a flourish and flush it down the toilet like so much cocaine. Then my parents would ship me off to some treatment center where I'd be put in group therapy with a bunch of Trekkies.

I would sit on my couch with the blinds drawn, stare at the TV screen, and imagine myself inside it. I wanted to cower in the dark brown rooms of Don Corleone, kiss his hand on his daughter's wedding day, explain what my troubles were, and let him tell me he'll make everything all right. Of course, I was prepared to accept this gift knowing that someday—and that day may never come—I may be called upon to do a service. But, he would tell me, "Until that day, accept this justice as a gift on my daughter's wedding day."

"*Grazie*, Godfather." It was as simple as that.

Looking back, I wonder why a gangster movie kidnapped my life. *The Godfather* had nothing to do with me. I was a feminist, not Italian, and I went to school at Montana State. I had never set foot in New York, thought ravioli came only in a can, and wasn't blind to the fact that all the women in the film were either virgins, mothers, whores, or Diane Keaton.

I fell for those made-up, sexist, East Coast thugs anyway. Partly it was the clothes; fashionwise, there is nothing less glamorous than snow-blown, backpacking college life in the Rocky Mountain states. But the thing that really attracted me to the film was that it offered a three-hour peep into a world with clear and definable moral guidelines; where you know where you stand and you know who you love; where honor was everything; and the greatest sin wasn't murder but betrayal.

My favorite scene in the film takes place on a deserted highway with the Statue of Liberty off in the distance. The don's henchman Clemenza is on the road with two of his men. He's under orders that only one of them is supposed to make the ride back. Clemenza tells the driver to

pull over. "I gotta take a leak," he says. As Clemenza empties his blad-
der, the man in the backseat empties his gun into the driver's skull.
There are three shots. The grisly, back-of-the-head murder of a rat
fink associate is all in a day's work. But Clemenza's overriding responsibility is to his family. He takes a moment out of his routine madness
to remember that he had promised his wife he would bring dessert
home. His instruction to his partner in crime is an entire moral mani-
festo in six little words: "Leave the gun. Take the cannoli."

I loved Clemenza's command because of its total lack of ambiguity. I
yearned for certainty. I'd been born into rock-solid Christianity, and
every year that went by, my faith eroded a little more, so that by the
time I got to college I was a recent, and therefore shaky, atheist. Like a
lot of once devout people who have lost religion, I had holes the size of
heaven and hell in my head and my heart. Once, I had had a god, commandments, faith, the promise of redemption, and a bible, The Bible,
which offered an explanation of everything from creation on through
to the end of the world. I had slowly but surely replaced the old-fashioned exclamation points of hallelujahs with the question marks of
modern life. God was dead and I had whacked him.

Don Corleone, the Godfather, was not unlike God the father—loving
and indulgent one minute, wrathful and judgmental the next. But the
only "thou shalt" in the don's dogma was to honor thy family. He
dances with his wife, weeps over his son's corpse, dies playing in the
garden with his grandson, and preaches that "a man who doesn't
spend time with his family can never be a real man."

Don Corleone would not have paid actual money to sit in fluorescent-lit rooms listening to frat boys from Spokane babble on about Descartes, boys in baseball caps whose most sacred philosophical motto could be summarized as "I drink therefore I am." Don Corleone had no time for mind games and conjecture. I, on the other hand, had nothing but time for such things, probably because I'm a frivolous female: "I spend my life trying not to be careless," the don tells his son Michael. "Women and children can be careless but not men."

The Godfather is a film crammed with rules for living. Don't bow down to big shots. It's good when people owe you. This drug business is dangerous. Is vengeance going to bring your son back to you or my boy to me? And then there is the grandeur, the finality, the conviction of the mantra "Never tell anybody outside the family what you're thinking again."

That last one was a rule I myself could follow. Not only did I not tell anyone outside my family what I was thinking, I was pretty tight-lipped with family too. If I was confused about the books I was reading in school, I was equally tormented by my seemingly tranquil life. At twenty-one, I was squandering my youth on hard work and contentment. I had two jobs, got straight A's. I lived with my boyfriend of three years, a perfectly nice person. We were well suited to the point of boredom, enjoying the same movies, the same music, the same friends. We didn't argue, which meant we didn't flirt. I'd always dreamed of *The Taming of the Shrew* and I was living in—well, they don't write dramas about young girls who settle for the adventure that is mutual respect, unless you count *thirtysomething*, and I already had the same haircut as the wifely actress who smiled politely waiting for her husband to come home to their comfortable house. Thanks largely to the boyfriend's decency and patience, my parents and I were getting along better than ever. My sister was my best friend. We all lived within ten blocks of each other, one big happy family, frequently convening for get-togethers and meals. Friends clamored for dinner invitations to my parents' home, acquaintances told the boyfriend and me that we renewed their faith in love, and every time I turned in an essay exam my professors' eyes lit up. I was a good daughter, a good sister, a good girlfriend, a good student, a good citizen, a responsible employee. I was also antsy, resentful, overworked, and hemmed in.

Just as I did not divulge my secret rendezvous with *The Godfather*, I didn't talk about my claustrophobia. I didn't tell anyone that maybe I didn't want to be known only as my sister's sister or my parents' daughter or my boyfriend's girlfriend, that maybe I'd lived in that town too long and I wanted to go someplace where I could leave the house for ten minutes without running into my seventh-grade math teacher. So I told them all I wanted to study abroad to better my chances of getting into graduate school, which sounds a lot better than telling the people who love you that you'd love to get away from them.

I have a few weeks after Christmas before I have to report to Holland for a semester of art history. I fly to Vienna. I get on a train there and another one in Berlin, and another after that, and one thing leads to another and I find myself in Italy. How did that happen? Oh well, as long as I'm in Florence, perhaps I should pop down and give Sicily a look-see.

The fact is, my little freedom flight isn't working out as well as I'd hoped. I swing between the giddiness of my newfound solitude and the loneliness of same. I make a lot of panicked phone calls to my boyfriend from museums that begin with descriptions of Brueghel paintings and end with me sobbing, "What am I going to do?" I am homesick, and since I can't go home, I might as well go to the next closest thing—Sicily. I *know* Sicily. And I love the part of *The Godfather* when Michael's hiding out, traipsing around his ancestral hills, walking the streets of his father's birthplace, Corleone.

I take a night train from Rome down the boot and wake up in the Sicilian capital, Palermo. I feel ridiculous. I thought of myself as a serious person and it didn't seem like serious people travel hundreds of miles out of their way to walk in the footsteps of Al Pacino.

I don't feel so silly, however, that I'm above tracking down a bakery and buying a cannoli, my first. I walk down to the sea and eat it. It's sweeter than I thought it would be, more dense. The filling is flecked with chocolate and candied orange. Clemenza was right: Leave that gun! Take that cannoli!

The town of Corleone really exists and can be reached by bus. I checked. Every day I go to the travel office in Palermo to buy a ticket to the Godfather's hometown. And every morning, when I stand before the ticket agent, I can never quite bring myself to say the word "Corleone" out loud to a real live Sicilian. Because you know they know. Idiot Americans and their idiot films. I have my dignity.

So each morning when the ticket agent asks, "Where to?", one of two things happens: I say nothing and just walk off and spend the day in Palermo reading John Irving novels on a bench by the sea, or I utter the name of a proper, art-historically significant town instead. As if the clerk will hear me say, "Agrigento," and say to himself, "Oh, she's going to see the Doric temple. Impressive. Wonder if she's free for a cannoli later?"

On my final day in Sicily—my last chance at Corleone—I walk to the ticket counter, look the clerk in the eye, and ask for a round-trip ticket to Corle—. . . Cefalù. Yeah, Cefalù, that's it, to see a Byzantine mosaic I remember liking in one of my schoolbooks.

Cefalù might as well have been Corleone. It had the same steep cobblestone streets and blanched little buildings that I remembered from the movie. *Lovely,* I thought, as I started walking up the hill to its tiny, twelfth-century cathedral. *Freak,* everyone in the town apparently thought as I marched past them. An entire class of schoolchildren stopped cold to gawk at me. Six-year-old girls pointed at my shoes and laughed. Hunched old men glared, as if the sight of me was a vicious insult. I felt like a living, breathing faux pas.

At least no one was inside the church. The only gaze upon me there came from the looming, sad-eyed Messiah. The Jesus in this mosaic is huge, three times larger than any other figure inside the church. And there's something menacing in the way he holds that tablet with the

word of God on it. But his face is compassionate. With that contradic-
tory mix of stern judgment and heart, he may as well have been wearing a tuxedo and stroking a cat and saying something like "What have I
ever done to make you treat me so disrespectfully?"

I leave the church and go for lunch. I am the patron in a tiny family
restaurant operated by Mama, Papa, Son 1, and Son 2. They glare at
me as if I glow in the dark. Soon they'll wish I glowed in the dark. The
power keeps going on and off because of a thunderstorm. The sky
outside is nearly black. The Muzak version of "A Whiter Shade of
Pale" is playing and it flickers, too, so that every few seconds it's dark
and silent. Which is a relief, considering that the rest of the time it's
loud and the entire family have seated themselves across from me
and gape without smiling. The eggplant on my plate is wonderful, but
such is my desire to escape their stares that I have never chewed so
fast in my life.

How had it never hit me before? The whole point of *The Godfather* is
not to trust anyone outside your family. And whatever I may have
thought while sitting in front of my VCR, I am not actually Sicilian. I
bear no resemblance to Clemenza, Tessio, or any of the heads of the
Five Families. If I were a character in the film at all, I'd be one of those
pain-in-the-ass innocent bystanders in the restaurant where Michael
murders Sollozzo. I'm the tuba player in Moe Green's casino. I'm that
kid who rides his bike past Michael and Kay on Kay's street in New
Hampshire who yells hello and neither Michael nor Kay says hello
back.

I got sucked in by *The Godfather*'s moral certainty, never quite recognizing that the other side of moral certainty is staying at home and keeping your mouth shut. Given the choice, I prefer chaos and confusion. Why live by those old-world rules? I was enamored of the movie's family ethos without realizing that in order to make a life for myself, I needed to go off on my own. Why not tell people outside the family what you're thinking? As I would later find out, it's a living.

Vindictively American

*Personally, I am too vindictively American, too full of
hate for the hateful aspects of this country, and too
possessed by the things I love here to be too long away.*

—RALPH ELLISON

MY FRIEND ESTHER BLAAUW AND I WERE WATCHING THE *ACHT UUR
Journaal*—Holland's eight o'clock television news. Emphasis on "watching." After three months at the University of Leiden, in April 1992, my Dutch vocabulary hadn't progressed much past *koffie, bier,* and "My name is Sarah how are you," words and phrases which didn't get much broadcast journalism airplay. The screen flashed pictures of buildings on fire. The newscaster said, "Dutch Dutch Dutch Dutch Dutch Los Angeles Dutch Dutch." I absentmindedly sighed, "Fires in southern California, what else is new?" But Esther turned her gaze from the TV set to stare at me. "What?" I asked, just as the newscaster said, "Dutch Dutch Dutch Rodney King."

Esther explained that a jury in Los Angeles had acquitted the four police officers accused of beating Rodney King. That surprised me, having seen the video. "Now," she said, "the whole city is on fire." That did not surprise me, having seen the video. Four people were dead from the mayhem. I stared at the smoky pictures. But Esther watched me, glaring at my hands accusingly, as if I could throw a brick through a shop window ten thousand miles away. She told me, only half joking, "Of course you're not going back there."

"Back where?" I asked.

"America." It sounded like a dirty word.

"I don't live in America," I said. "I live in Montana." I smirked a little, thinking of my hometown, in which the police report tends to consist of cute items like somebody walking past The Paint Pot on Main Street called in to say they noticed through the window that a coffeemaker had been left on. Not exactly Florence and Normandie.

Still, Esther wouldn't drop it. "Why would you ever want to go back *there*?" she scowled, waving at the TV, where a palm tree was in flames.

"Because it's huge" was the only thing I could come up with.

I wished that I could describe the hugeness. That it wasn't just a huge mess. I wanted to tell Esther about the Montana sky and how it's so gigantic that Montana is called Big Sky Country and how I missed it so much I pretended that behind the constant Dutch ceiling of clouds there was a big range of mountains with snow way up top. I wanted to tell her that even though I liked being twenty minutes away from Amsterdam, I was the kind of person who will sit in a car for the thirteen-hour drive to Seattle—for Esther the equivalent of driving to Greece—just to see a band I like. I wanted to tell her that every time I meet her for some dinky thimbleful of coffee in the student union I daydream about big steaming diner cups and so many free refills you can't help but talk real fast.

I wanted to tell her that looking at those riots on TV was digging a hole inside me and could she try and understand. But I ran out of there. I didn't have the heart to try and explain why my lunatic homeland was going up in smoke to a resident of that sane little country whose craziest cultural brouhaha had been the great tulip mania of 1636. I jumped on my little bike and rode through the little town past a couple of little windmills. I went up to my little room and fell to pieces.

I finally fell asleep after listening to a Beach Boys song about twenty-nine times on my Walkman—"Wouldn't It Be Nice." Wouldn't it be nice if four people weren't dead because four other people mauled their fellow citizen with billy clubs, over and over and over again? Wouldn't it be nice if all those men and women weren't running onto freeways and shooting guns in the air and shooting guns at each other and looting TV sets out of stores and being teargassed and terrorized and slain? Wouldn't it be nice if that truck driver wasn't lying in some hospital bed barely hanging on because a mob tore him out of his truck and attacked him en masse? Justice, wouldn't that be nice? I guess I needed to hear towheaded California boys singing something so beautiful and so sappy as "Maybe if we think and wish and hope and pray it might come true." The song ends "Sleep tight my baby." I kept rewinding that part.

Wasn't that why I was in Holland anyway, to get some rest, to take a break from the chaos? It just so happened I decided to leave the country during the Gulf War, an action I didn't understand then and don't understand much better now called for by a president I did not vote for once and would not vote for again. Studying abroad required a lengthy application process. I remember the exchange program office organized a seminar on anti-American sentiment a few weeks after smart bombs were dropping into Iraq. We had to sit in a circle and they asked each one of us, "What would you do if you were abroad and some foreigners came up to you and expressed anti-American sentiment?"

"Agree with them," I said.

I think I wrote on my exchange program application that I wanted to study in the Netherlands to do research on the paintings of Piet Mondrian, but I didn't say why the paintings of Piet Mondrian appealed to me. Those paintings were clean little grids, immaculate white rectangles and perfect black lines brightened by cheerful, childlike squares of red, yellow, and blue. They symbolized a real kinder, gentler country—Holland—a place of universal health care, efficient public transportation, a well-educated citizenry, and merry villages crammed with bicycles and flowers and canals. I wanted out of the huge Jackson Pol-

lock canvas that is the U.S.A., vast, murky, splotched, and slapped together by a drunk.

I got to do my Mondrian research all right, but when I showed up in
Leiden I was told the art history courses I came to take "happened last
semester." Not speaking Dutch, in order to stay—and keep my finan-
cial aid—I had to sign up for some random classes in the languages I do
speak, English and French. The low point was registering for a literature course called Vision on America During the '80s. Great. Like I
crossed the Atlantic to pay nineteen dollars for a Jay McInerney pa-
perback. I came all this way to the land of bread-for-breakfast for the
grand purpose of explaining to my classmates that this thing called
Count Chocula in Thomas Pynchon's *Vineland* is a chocolate-flavored
cereal with a vampire theme. Luckily, I loved the teacher, Professor
d'Haen, who glowed a little when recalling his student days in some—
to him—romantic place like Ohio or Pennsylvania.

Just before the riots we'd read Don DeLillo's *White Noise* from 1985,
a book I had liked mainly because a character in it had a thing for Elvis.
But the morning after I heard about Los Angeles, I dove into that book
as a talisman of truth, rereading it in a single sitting, eerily noticing
the claim that "we need catastrophe" and that "this is where California
comes in." I relived its "airborne toxic event," its insistence that "all
plots tend to move deathward," its fixation on a thousand cheap
American details—the supermarket shelves and the cars we drive and
the food we eat in the cars we drive.

And I wept. I tossed all my Mondrian books on the floor and hugged that apocalyptic American novel to my chest and rocked back and forth, missing all of it, death and Elvis and California and catastrophe. I wanted Jackson Pollock. And I wanted to go home. I got on my bike and rode to McDonald's and read the book again, smearing its pages with fries.

These Little Town Blues

*People used to tell me that to be a success I should say
I was from New York City.*

— BRUCE SPRINGSTEEN

AN ACQUAINTANCE OF MINE HAS CONVINCED HIMSELF THAT AMERICAN popular music ends with Frank Sinatra. To him, Sinatra is the apogee of adult cool, and all the pop stars après Frank are kid stuff—scraggly, talentless, unformed. I don't agree, but I can see his point. No one, not even Beck, ever looked that good in a suit.

Apart from Elvis Presley, Frank Sinatra is the most towering musical figure this century, and this country, have produced. His complicated, love-him/hate-him persona and his twisting, turning road map of a voice are nearly as large as America itself. Which is why one Sinatra fan can decide he's the end of an era and another can argue he's where it all begins. And so in my bible, Frank Sinatra is not Revelation; he's Genesis, where pop starts. Frank Sinatra is the first punk.

Punk is rhythm, style, poetry, comedy, defiance, and, above all, ambition. Punk is wounded. It's what happened to Frank Sinatra's voice after Ava Gardner broke his heart. Punk means moral indignation. It's the way Frank Sinatra, tired of getting screwed by Capitol Records, told its president, "Fuck you, and fuck your building." Punk means the self-determination required to start your own record company, Reprise, as in reprisal, so that you can do what you want. Punk means getting all worked up. It's being able to make the shockingly simple line in "Angel Eyes" about how "the laugh's on me" into the world's most devastating portrait of sadness. Punk is female, which is why the bravest punks are either women or womanly men. Would there have been a Kurt Cobain wearing his ball gown on MTV's *Headbanger's Ball* if there had been no Sinatra, who, Steve Erickson wrote, "made America accept the idea of a man singing like a woman without sounding like one"? Best of all, punk comes out of nowhere. Punk is a torch that's passed around, a rumor that spreads from one nowhere to another that guts and perseverance mean more than anything else.

My American punk top ten in no particular order: Jerry Lee Lewis from Nowhere, Louisiana; Richard Hell from Nowhere, Kentucky; Bob Dylan from Nowhere, Minnesota; the Fastbacks, Nirvana, and Sleater-Kinney from Nowhere, Washington; Patti Smith, Bruce Springsteen, Allen Ginsberg, and Frank Sinatra from Nowhere, New Jersey. Perhaps it's coincidence that forty percent of my list are Garden State flowers, but I don't think so. Punk comes out of nowhere and where's more no than there? This is the state Paterson native Ginsberg called "nowhere Zen New Jersey"; the place Freehold homeboy Springsteen referred to as a "dump"; the place South Jerseyan Smith described in her song "Piss Factory"; the place, it is said, that even Sinatra has called a "sewer." Or, as my guidebook puts it, the state "has a superb interstate highway system for a reason."

Hoboken, New Jersey, Sinatra's hometown, doesn't feel like a place. It feels like a symbol. To be in Hoboken is to experience in three-dimensional form America's admiration of and alienation from New York. If you grow up in any other Nowhere, U.S.A., you might be aware that New Yorkers look down their noses at you, but at least out there in the dark fields of the republic you don't have to stare straight up their nostrils every time you walk outside. Because the first thing you notice about Hoboken is Manhattan. If you look across the Hudson from downtown Hoboken, New York City's sharp-toothed skyline bites you in the neck. To your immediate New Jersey right is a humble little old joint called the Clam Broth House. To your left is the World Trade Center, the Empire State Building, and all the other big-shot towers of babble assembled in a united front of taunting: *What are YOU looking at?*

Facing Manhattan from Hoboken is reminiscent of one other American vantage point: the view from Alcatraz. As on the Rock, you stand and gaze across the water at a glittering city-on-a-hill and feel like trash, like they're good and you're not, like if you had any guts at all you'd risk death and swim across that river right now.

"I want to be a part of it," proclaims Hoboken's most famous son in the theme from *New York New York.* "Those little town blues are melting away," he swaggers. It's not Frank's best song, but it's a very old, very satisfying story. He made it there. He made it everywhere.

You would like to think that Hoboken, New Jersey, brags about Frank Sinatra at sickening length. You would like to imagine that every last site where the forming Frank spit his gum out would be marked with a plaque. You would like walking tours and history. You would like to stand before the nondescript brown row house at 841 Garden Street, where Frank lived between the ages of sixteen and twenty-three, and read some sort of fanciful marker with a speculative text gushing, "This is the place where our beloved Frank Sinatra spent his late adolescence and young-adult years. And since this period is the incubator of desire, this is the stoop where the young man must have plotted his escape. Push the button to hear 'Street of Dreams.' " You want the drama of Graceland, but you don't even get the tragedy of Tupelo. Just a normal, unmarked house with a baby stroller in the entry and recycling bins downstairs in a regular middle-class enclave.

From this oversight, you get the feeling that Hoboken is having a hard time celebrating itself—and having a harder time fitting its most famous son into its story. This has something to do with the fact that its most famous son left. "Frank turned his back on Hoboken," third-generation Hobokenite Robin Shamburg tells me. And who could blame him? At his first big public homecoming, during the town's Italian American Day in 1948, his former paisanos threw rocks at the stage. "They shat on him," Shamburg continues. Still, some Hobokenites hardly mind that their prodigal son has largely avoided the town through the years. "There are certain diehard fans who gloss over that fact," she says. "They idolize him."

That idolatry is on display, albeit in understated Hoboken fashion, at Sinatra's birthplace at 415 Monroe Street. The blocks leading up to it are meaner, shabby. You get there, and it's not there. The building where the newborn Frankie belted his very first song of life burned down. In its place is a monument, the saddest possible brick arch, with wooden doors below it to block the view of an empty lot. No triumphal arch for this Jersey Justinian, no ornate relief carvings of his Oscar triumphs, his gold records, his pals or his gals. Just a plain stack of unadorned bricks. A comparatively snazzy blue-and-gold star marks the sidewalk in front of it. "Francis Albert Sinatra," it reads. "The Voice, Born Here at 415 Monroe Street, December 12, 1915." You'd step on it if you weren't looking down.

Tell it to the town planners: All the birthplace site really needs to spiff up its ambience is a loudspeaker. Frank's voice can make any old shack feel luxurious. Witness the scene at the architecturally modest Piccolo's, a delightful all-Sinatra, all-the-time cheesesteak dive on Clinton Street, established in 1955. The joint blares a constant Sinatra sound track, inside and out. As I walk up to it for lunch one Friday, the first thing I hear from down the street is "Although I may not be the man some girls think of as handsome." This line from "Someone to Watch Over Me" is completely ironic given Frank's angel eyes, but the voice singing it is a slow, warm kiss.

It helps if you're hungry more for myth than for food at Piccolo's. The fare is midcentury American, greasy but handmade. The grill is manned by a bunch of good-humored guys in white hats chopping at cheesesteaks and cooking up french fries hot enough to burn your tongue. I slip into the back room. The walls are crammed with framed photos, most of which are of Sinatra. The highlight is a proud photograph from the November 6, 1986, issue of *The Jersey Journal* that shows the exterior of Piccolo's plastered with a giant sign reading, "It's All Right Mr. Sinatra, We Love You, That Book Lies!", a reference to local disdain for Kitty Kelley's unauthorized biography *His Way*.

To refute "that book" is the reason Hoboken's Ed Shirak Jr. wrote *Our Way: In Honor of Frank Sinatra*, which you can pick up at Lepore's Home Made Chocolates, the Garden Street candy store Shirak owns with partner Mario Lepore. Shirak writes that his fellow citizens "were incensed by 'that book' as if it had disgraced the town." If Hoboken deplores hubbub—disdaining Kelley's book while at the same time not exactly going out of its way to honor Sinatra either—Ed Shirak is a one-man band, embarking on his story (which lists some of Shirak's Sinatra tourism dreams and schemes) after reading "the first forty-four pages of Kitty Kelley's book" and vowing to "simply tell the truth." The self-published *Our Way* reads like a book-length fanzine, which is to say that the joy of it lies in the author's personal account of Sinatra's life as seen through the prism of fandom and hometown pride. Shirak twice ran for mayor of Hoboken and lost. How can you not vote for a guy who, when he worked in New York in his twenties, would tell people, "I'm from Hoboken, home of Frank Sinatra"?

Shirak's narrative swerves from his family's history in Hoboken to that of the Sinatras, from Shirak's political campaigns to his desperate attempts to present Frank Sinatra with the tribute song he wrote with his friends. The song, "A Time That Was," tells the story of Frank's Hoboken youth. A tape comes free when you purchase *Our Way* at Lepore's Home Made Chocolates.

A time that was? Was what? According to the saccharine lyrics, the past was simpler, full of flags, parades, and familial love. Once upon a time, an ambitious lad walked among them. The remarkable thing about "A Time That Was" isn't so much the lyrics ("He walked the streets in a young boy's dream, trying to make it on his own") or the old-fashioned melody, which begs for string accompaniment. What's striking is Shirak's *need* for Sinatra to hear it. Shirak's mantra is a phrase he overheard once: "Nobody gets to Sinatra, nobody." There have been a few touching near misses, duly recorded in the book. Shirak and Lepore go to a Sinatra concert at the Sands in Atlantic City, serendipitously finding themselves in the restaurant where Frank is having his preshow meal. Of course, when Shirak approaches his idol, bodyguards whisk Sinatra away. The two Hobokenites still love the show, but it must hurt a little when their hometown hero closes with—what else?—"New York, New York."

Sinatra eventually hears the song. But with Shirak's luck, it's only after his book has gone to press. Which is why the book's denouement is Shirak's introduction to his cassette: He reads aloud the letter he received from Sinatra that says, "What a nice tribute."

The most stunning item in Shirak's pages is a photograph he found in his parents' basement. It is such a perfectly symbolic image, you can hardly believe it exists as a physical object. It pictures a young, frail Frank Sinatra sitting cross-legged on the boardwalk in Hoboken, looking across the Hudson at Manhattan. The boy's gaunt face wears a mask of resolve. He leans forward, but just slightly, as if he is on the verge of standing up, as if his gangly arms and legs are willing themselves to that place where his heart already is. It is difficult, after you see that haunting portrait, to imagine the young Frank Sinatra as anything other than Gatsby staring at the green light at the end of the pier.

You forget that there are still folks in this town who knew Sinatra as a young man (a very well-dressed young man, of course, but still resolutely one of them). Leo DiTerlizzo, of Leo's Grandevous, is such a person. Walking into his bar at Second and Grand on a Saturday night is like stepping into a fan letter. The walls of this comfortable, broken-in room are covered with dozens of framed images of Frank, including an especially aw-shucks shot of the singer holding a puppy, and an unintentionally grotesque green painting of him which lords over a jukebox dominated by his CDs. Leo is the owner, the bartender, and a boyhood friend of Frank's. He tells me that the man himself has sat at this bar on two occasions, that he has visited Leo's home upstairs, and that Leo just spoke to him by telephone two weeks earlier and that Frank's feeling fine. Leo is a lovely, soft-spoken man who never stops moving behind the bar, filling drinks and joking with the waitresses, shuffling around to his old friend's voice.

Unfortunately, Jimmy Buffett's "Margaritaville" was on when I came inside, but a few quarters later I got my faves, like "That's Life" and "I Get a Kick out of You" and, of course, "Saturday Night (Is the Loneliest Night of the Week)." Who says happiness never comes cheap? A jukebox stocked with Sinatra can turn your world around.

I ask Leo if the woman standing next to Frank in the photograph over the bar is Dolly, Sinatra's locally infamous mother. Leo responds, "That's my wife." (Obviously, years of listening to Sinatra haven't made me any more suave.) I ask him what his favorite song is and put it on the jukebox as an apology. It's "Summer Wind," a song I've heard a thousand times, which does not mean that I ever paid attention. You can live with a tune for years and it never seeps in; it just lingers, waiting to be noticed. Normally, I prefer the Frank extremes—either vainglorious or defeated, the macho thrill of "Come Dance with Me" or that rock-bottom classic "When No One Cares."

"Summer Wind" is an in-between song. It's relaxed, seductive. The arrangement is perfect, the voice sexy and dear. Frank's old pal Leo, who has been married for fifty-nine years, sways ever so slightly to its pretty pulse, occasionally mouthing the words. Watching him, watching what looks to be a picture of contentment, makes you wonder about the man Frank Sinatra might have been if he had never crossed the river, if he had never sung this song. Maybe he would still be married to the mother of his children. Maybe he would be as blissful as this hardworking Leo appears to be, though where would that leave

Leo, not to mention the rest of us? We would all be doomed to waste away in one stifling Margaritaville after another with no sweet, blue breeze on our skin. Leo says, "I go upstairs, and I go to sleep, and I dream Sinatra."

If you were born Somebody, you might expect that. You might expect starring roles in other people's dreams. If you were born Somewhere, hubris would come easy. But if you are Nowhere's child, hubris is an import, pride a thing you decide to acquire. That's what all the punks know. That's why a cocksure Patti Smith could cover "So You Want to Be a Rock 'n' Roll Star" and sound as if she wrote the song herself. That's why the then completely unknown Corin Tucker of Sleater-Kinney could sing "I'm the queen of rock and roll" and make you believe her. And it's why you buy the chutzpah of Hoboken's Frank Sinatra when he sings a silly song like "New York, New York" and tells you he'll be "top of the heap." One thing punk—and Sinatra especially—never does is take that kind of self-confidence for granted. Because anyone who comes from Nowhere knows how easy it would be to go right back.

Chelsea Girl

HERE ARE TWO STATUES OF LIBERTY IN NEW YORK—THE ONE FOR IMMIGRANTS out on Liberty Island, and the one for weirdos at 222 West Twenty-third Street. One might imagine that the marker tacked onto the Chelsea Hotel's Victorian facade proclaims, "Give me your junkies, your geniuses, your men in eye makeup, yearning to lay low." But the real sign lacks any Emma Lazarus pizzazz. It straightforwardly announces that the historic landmark "opened in 1884 as one of the city's earliest cooperative apartment houses," became a hotel in 1905, and has been the refuge of the relatively respectable literary lights O. Henry, Dylan Thomas, and Thomas Wolfe. (What? You were expecting they'd advertise Sid Vicious?)

The list of Chelsea residents past is so impressive as to appear fictitious. Mark Twain slept here. Arthur C. Clarke wrote *2001: A Space Odyssey* here. Robert Mapplethorpe showed up with his lover Patti Smith, way back in the days when Robert Mapplethorpe would have had a lover named Patti. Teen movie actress Gaby Hoffmann of *Sleepless in Seattle* semifame spent her childhood here with her mother, Viva, the Warhol Superstar. American folk chronicler and filmmaker Harry Smith wiggled his way around a room bursting with his collections of Ukrainian Easter eggs and Seminole dresses. Depending on your theory of what happened in Room 100, Sid Vicious killed Nancy Spungen here, or Nancy killed herself, or somebody broke in and killed Nancy, leaving Sid to take the blame. Bob Dylan was here in the mid-'60s, around his *Blonde on Blonde* heyday, flirting with Edie Sedgwick, whose amphetamines and pearls he may or may not have been singing about in "Just Like a Woman." And thanks to Dylan Thomas, who drank himself to death here, and Sedgwick, the It-Girl-turned-burn-victim who set her room on fire, it is the only hotel I can think of where people unfamiliar with New York know the name of the nearest hospital—St. Vincent's—because the phrase "rushed to St. Vincent's" tends to pop up in Chelsea lore.

At the Chelsea, famous and infamous are often confused, as are eccentricity and crime. The anything-goes atmosphere isn't without its hazards. Arthur Miller, one of the great moralists of the American century, spent much of the '60s living here, attending what he calls the "ceaseless Chelsea party." In his autobiography, *Timebends*, Miller describes walking into the lobby back then and encountering an agitated young woman handing out leaflets which outlined her ambition to shoot a man, any man. He writes, "I said to the management that this woman was going to kill somebody and maybe something ought to be done about her before she exploded, but she was a member of the party, it seemed, and it wouldn't do to be too square about it." Which was too bad for a certain Pope of Pop; the woman turned out to be Valerie Solanas, and she shot a man (sort of) named Andy Warhol in 1968.

The Chelsea seems to attract all the best people—the best painters, the best singers, the best killers. Its appeal is a mystery. For who knows what lies in the heart of a place—a few rooms in a fairly crummy part of town—that became a beacon to so many tattered troubadours. Any old youth hostel could harbor penniless punks. But composer Virgil Thomson, too? And Arthur Miller, he of the Pulitzer prize? What gives?

Though the Chelsea's rep is that of a dorm of the dispossessed, it is a hotel, with rooms and reservations and check-ins and everything. I show up on the Fourth of July as an Arthur Miller joke. As Miller wrote about the hotel, "It was not part of America, had no vacuum cleaners, no rules, no taste, no shame." True to form, on our national holiday, it has no red, no white, no blue. That night, as I return from watching fireworks around midnight, I make some quip to a man who lives on my floor like, "Well, well, another year for our nation." He says, "For your nation maybe. Me, I celebrate Canada Day." It was the sort of treasonous claptrap I should have expected from this embassy of insurgents.

Such are the random encounters of the Chelsea Hotel: One minute you're bathing in the aura of Dylan Thomas, the next minute you're drowning in sticky goo. One afternoon a friend and I are sitting in the lobby. A woman who lives in the hotel sits in a chair next to us. She proceeds to transport the contents of a cup of lemonade into a bottle, the reverse of the standard bottle-to-cup operating procedure. Of course lemonade and ice spill everywhere, all over the floor, all over the table next to us. When she catches us staring at her mess, she justifies it, harping, "You think this is a mess? New York is a mess! Why should it matter if I spill anything inside? The whole city is a dump! I'm not pretending the inside is any different than the outside anymore!"

Away from the lobby's camaraderie, the Chelsea's public gangways—the elevators, the stairwell, the halls—are among the creepiest psychic spaces in town. I didn't want to let down my guard, let myself relax, almost as if I were still out on the street keeping my wits about me. Maybe it's because I know the late William S. Burroughs used to haunt, I mean live, here, but I can't shake the watch-your-back imperative: as if, any second, Burroughs, or someone similarly croaky, will creak open one of the doors and tap my shoulder with the bony hand of death. And after a staredown with a disquieting ghoul in the elevator, I start taking the stairs down, racing past flight after flight hung with the brushstrokes of madmen that are the tenants' paintings, giving a whole new meaning to the phrase "bad hotel art."

The botanical beauty of the stairs' famous ironwork would be well worth a lingering look, but every time I leave my room, a voice in my head whispers, *Keep it moving.*

My room, marked 923 in ballpoint on a crumbling index card taped to the door, is an Edward Hopper painting waiting to happen. So Hopperesque, in fact, that upon entering I feel a need to put on a grimy old slip and slump into the dusty armchair so that I can stare wantonly at the wall. The drapes are caked with enough dirt to house a medium-size ant farm; the rug is salted with the dander of life; the bathroom might have crumbled but for the architectural support offered by other people's hair. Though the television has cable (a new development), the remote control does not work. Another concession to progress, a professional hotel telephone, exists for the sole purpose of receiving other guests' voice mail, several of whom were invited to a Brooklyn barbecue at "the Delgados' " on the Fourth, not that they would ever find out. And taking up most of the counter space of the "kitchenette" is a hot plate— is there a sadder appliance on the face of the earth?—pining for ramen, soup cans, and other suicide food. At least I end up facing Twenty-third Street: Dylan Thomas got stuck in a dark room at the back on his final trip and everybody knows what happened to him.

I'm no neat freak. It's just that, like a lot of people from working-class backgrounds, I don't particularly romanticize squalor. Just because I have dirty little books by Jean Genet on my shelves at home, doesn't mean there aren't cleaning products labeled "antibacterial" under the sink.

At the Chelsea, I know from the first night that my impulse to wear shoes at all times I'm not in bed is sound when my left sneaker crunches down on something as I'm talking on the phone. A quick, horrified glance down at my foot reveals the roommate who would keep me company for my entire five-day boho holiday: a condom wrapper, empty. I consider throwing it away, but that would require touching it.

Often in hotels, I entertain myself falling asleep imagining my room's past occupants. Were there honeymooners? Lonesome businessmen? One-night stands? Incognito Sally Field–type mothers on the lam from abusive husbands? In anonymous hotels, anything could have happened. At the Chelsea, I'm armed with too much information. History is a two-way street. I wanted to stay here because it's where Patti Smith was getting her act together on the verge of her album *Horses*, where Mark Twain cracked wise, where William Burroughs was up to God knows what. But every night when I turn off the light, all I can think of is Nancy Spungen's blood, seeping.

In Alex Cox's biopic *Sid and Nancy*, the ex–Sex Pistols bassist and his bleach-blond girlfriend get kicked from one Chelsea room to another thanks to fire (Sid never got famous for originality, and in '78 blazes at the Chelsea were so '65). In the movie's best line, the bellman looks Sid in the eye and piously intones, "Bob Dylan was born here." Though patently untrue (as Virgil Thomson said about his once neighbor in Jean Stein's *Edie*, Dylan "is a perfectly nice Jewish high-school graduate from Hibbing, Minnesota, who speaks correctly and with manners"), there's a cosmic veracity to the whopper.

Could all these Who's Whos just be drawn to the building? "I would like to think that management had something to do with it," grins

manager Stanley Bard. If the Chelsea is a cuckoo's nest, Bard is its
anti–Nurse Ratched, a trim, deadpan man with melancholy eyes. He's
considerate, congenial, and inordinately proud of the hotel, proud of
its clientele. Indeed, despite the hotel's reputation for bohemian ex-
cess, Bard has an air of what can only be called respectability. How can
such an upstanding man tend this barnyard of black sheep? Then
again, Bard's inherent straight-arrow work ethic must be the reason
the Chelsea manages to remain standing no matter how many Edies
there are about to burn it down. His smallish frame is a formidable
wall for all the crazy balls to bounce off.

If there is one story to be gleaned from the Chelsea Hotel, it is the
story of tolerance, even when tolerance isn't necessarily called for. It
is the story of one family, a dynasty now, three generations in an increasingly homogenous, multinational, corporate world who, through
passion, a sense of history, and long hours, remain resolutely local,
personal, and, for better or worse, unique. Says singer Debbie Harry,
who frequented the place during her Blondie days, "I think it's a mir-
acle it hasn't been taken over by Ramada or something."

The Chelsea is strictly mom-and-pop. Or, more precisely, father
and son. Stanley Bard's father David took over the hotel in 1939. Stanley Bard came on in 1957, assuming management in 1964, when his
father died. Bard calls the Chelsea his father's "second child." He says
that as a little boy—he was five the first time he set foot in the Chelsea—
he was often jealous of his architectural sibling: "My mother would
drag me down here as a little child to see him." ("I used to love to ride

the lift," he says, proving that he is, in effect, now working in what used to be his playground.) But in those days, his father worked "fifteen to twenty hours a day." Which didn't stop him from putting his own children through the same form of orphanhood when he took over. "I'm here very often twelve to fifteen hours every day," he sighs. And now he runs the place with his son, David, who has worked here for nearly a decade.

Stanley Bard talks about his tenants with paternal pride. He boasts, "I've had the pleasure of knowing these people, knowing them well, and seeing their development." He sounds more like a guidance counselor from *Fame* than a service-industry bureaucrat. "I try to understand their needs," he says. "We're very compassionate. Creative people need that. They need to feel that they're being considered; they need to feel that they are happy in their surroundings." Three decades of dealing with the freakier angels and devils of our culture has left Bard bilingual in English and Artspeak. Not that I've chatted up that many hotel managers, but I can't imagine many of them throwing around the terminology of painting as nonchalantly as Stanley Bard. "I've seen all the movements," he points out. "The pop movement. The neorealistic movement."

When Bard names names, he breaks his famous tenants down by medium. You can tell he's rattled off the list so often and so fast that he's stitched each discipline into one huge Frankensteinian art monster. "Just in painting and sculpture," he chirps, "deKooningDavidSmithJasperJohnsLarryRiversChristo. And in act-ing, SarahBernhardtJaneFondaElliottGouldKrisKristofferson. A lot of nice people."

It's obvious that one of the joys of Bard's job is the intellectual challenge involved in thirty years of keeping up his end of the conversation. "Christo was a person who I really didn't understand. He wrapped everything in his room. One of his early works: He used to wrap his wife, Jeanne-Claude. A beautiful woman. And I said, 'Christo, I don't understand. What are you trying to say?' Because I used to question everyone. They felt sorry for me and my lack of knowledge. He said, 'You look at a woman and you just accept her. They're really beautiful objects. So what better way could I do by showing my art by wrapping a beautiful woman?' "

Something tells me they aren't having this conversation over at the Grand Hyatt uptown.

I find myself staring at that condom wrapper every time I am in the room. I keep humming Leonard Cohen's song "Chelsea Hotel #2," his supposed ode to Janis Joplin. Its beginning is sweet enough—"I remember you well in the Chelsea Hotel"—then gets rather to the point: "Giving me head on the unmade bed." Gosh. Call me picky, but after nearly a week with someone else's sexual detritus, I decide that Cohen's word-picture is fine enough subject matter for a pop song but not fine at all as a situation, as a fact of hostelry.

After I get over the initial gross-out, my bourgeois alarm goes off. Am I being too middle class? A prude? Of course, in any other hotel, I'd call the front desk immediately to complain. But staying at the

Chelsea necessarily involves a certain self-reflection. In other words, if this was good enough for Arthur Miller, shouldn't it be good enough for the lesser likes of me? When Miller wrote that the Chelsea was outside of America, didn't he mean outside of McCarthyite America? The bad one? That "no vacuum cleaners, no rules" bit of his—wasn't that a slam against all that is small-minded and neatnik and shackled? Like, isn't my preconception that this erotic garbage should have been thrown away before my arrival a . . . rule, man?

When I tell journalist Lance Loud, a former Chelsea denizen, about the wrapper on the floor, he laughs the guffaw of recognition: "As opposed to most hotels where they go around and clean the rooms, I'm sure the [Chelsea] maids go around from room to room and leave the used condoms and wrinkle up the sheets and blow their noses on the washcloths just so you know that that price you're paying is for genuine, New York circa-the-sixties cachet, no matter how germ-ridden it might be."

Loud, who has the distinction of being one of the first persons to come out on national television, moved to the Chelsea in 1971. It was during the filming of *An American Family*, a proto–*Real World* PBS documentary series which followed Lance's Santa Barbara family for a year. The first episode shows an under-the-weather Lance phoning home from his "crummy pad in New York" at the Chelsea, asking his sister to "send me my scarves."

"My first contact with the Chelsea Hotel," he recalls, "was as a rabid teenager from suburban southern California who was reading

anything he could about the strange and exotic state of mind called
Andy Warhol, which seemed so anarchic and so far away and so contrary to everything I knew." Then he saw Warhol's film *The Chelsea
Girls*, a split-screen, three-and-a-half-hour bore/smut fest, which
shows things like Ondine shooting speed and Nico in tears. Its
poster, a nude woman-as-hotel in which the Chelsea's entrance is
situated at her vagina, was like some exotic travel brochure to Lance
Loud. To him, it was his dream destination: "Some people want to go
to Valhalla. Some people want to go to El Dorado or Shangri-La.
When I was a teenager, I wanted to end up at the Chelsea Hotel. With
or without a needle in my arm and lipstick on my face." He arrived at
the hotel as the kept companion of a psychotic drug addict. Who says
dreams can't come true?

"I was terrified," Loud recalls. "It's one thing to dream about this
Gothic mansion of debauchery," he says. "But it's another thing for a
fairly innocent young urchin from the suburbs to come and actually
stay there." He's grateful for the experience: "I don't want to be a
bummer about it. You got the feeling that it was full of a lot of disembodied people who were on the road to some other reality. Purgatory
is a cathartic thing. The best parts of life sometimes are kill or cure."

Actually, though Loud's tale is almost comically grim, it does get to
the heart of the Chelsea's noir appeal. The Chelsea isn't so much a hotel as a hideout, a refuge, a hospice. It is said that Loud's then neighbor
Patti Smith ended up here, cradling an ill Robert Mapplethorpe in her
arms, because she could think of nowhere else to go, could imagine no

other sanctuary in New York for a couple of down-and-out oddballs who, like so many, happened to have big dreams but no money, hoping that the Chelsea would take them in. Stanley Bard welcomed them: "I liked them. They were nice, honest people who came to me and said they had no money and someday they would. Would I trust them and go along with them? Yes."

Who doesn't crave a little refuge (or a loan) at least once in life, especially when you're young and broke, or old and broke, or moving up, or slipping away? People don't always need, don't always want, a clean well-lighted place. As an outsider passing through, the Chelsea felt like a lonely place, solitary and sad. But the nice thing about loneliness (and solitude and sadness) is the silence. The Chelsea is a very quiet place to think. And this could be its secret, its attraction for those with poems and pictures rattling round their heads. It is an oasis of hush in one the noisiest cities on earth. And the silence isn't just spiritual—it's real, technological; the Chelsea has the thickest of walls. In fact, one of my neighbors during my stay was English comedian Eddie Izzard, in town doing his one-man show *Dress to Kill*. In it, he had a bit about how he loved the hotel's dense walls because he could scream all he wanted at his computer, said he sat in his room every night yelling, "Log on! Log on! Log on! LOG ON!" No one ever heard a peep.

Arthur Miller, for a while, evidently found the less-than-sanitary site cathartic. "The Chelsea," he wrote, "for all its irritants—the age-old dust in its drapes and carpets [corroboration!], the rusting pipes, the leaking refrigerator, the air conditioner into which you had to keep pouring pitchers of water—was an impromptu, healing ruin."

There is one man who has given a lot of thought to renovating the ruin—Stanley Bard's son David. Like his father, David hopes to pass the hotel on to his children. Unlike his father, he's caught in the middle between the place's past and tourism's future. A handsome, soft-spoken man in his thirties, David Bard is not unaware of the Chelsea's facilities (or lack thereof). This is a person who knows full well other hotels this size offer little bottles of shampoo, for instance. Or room service. Or minibars. This is the person responsible for the new phone system, for cable TV.

It is doubtful that even the shiniest of gadgets thoughtfully plopped into the hotel's rooms will outshine the glare of its grandly sad stories. This fact alone might prevent the kind of bourgeois, Disney-fired renovation taking place a few blocks north in Times Square. When I ask David Bard if he even thinks it's possible to Disney up Dylan Thomas, all he does is laugh. "No. Or Mapplethorpe." That kind of revamp would turn the sad stories merely sick. What would there be? A Do Not Go Gentle into That Good Nightclub? Would there be an Arthur Miller–themed Death of a Salesman Business Center, equipped with computers and fax machines? A Sid and Nancy Honeymoon Suite?

In fact, what happened to Sid and Nancy's room is a testament to how the Bards have dealt with the darker side that sometimes comes with the territory. Stanley Bard effectively destroyed Room 100 as an act of honor. He says of the killing, "Unfortunately we have to accept it. It's history and it did happen. I did not want it to become a legend for that reason. So we incorporated it into a large apartment which is now quite lovely. A very nice artist is living in that apartment." And so the Bard family receives a few measly bucks from a nice artist instead of raking in the tourist dollars of rubbernecking necros.

And if young David Bard gets his way, major makeovers won't be happening any time soon. Sitting in front of a shelf that contains one of my college art history textbooks, David talks about his early, more difficult years at the hotel. "When I first got out of college," he remembers, "I had this idea of literally gutting the building and renovating it and making everything clean corners, like a modern situation." How alluring. How un-Chelsea. "A couple of the artists in the building, they said to me, 'David, you don't want to get rid of the cracks and the crevices in the building because that's where the ghosts hide. And if you get rid of the ghosts, the Chelsea will just be any other building.' "

Michigan and Wacker

HAD THIS THEORY, A CHICAGO THEORY. AFTER FOUR YEARS OF WALKING BACK and forth across the Michigan Avenue Bridge, I had accumulated a few random facts about the bridge that coalesced into an actual hypothesis. Namely, that I could tell the whole history of America standing on that bridge. I thought I might be able to swivel around and point at the whole dark, inspiring tale. I had the following tidbits to go on: a couple of French explorers who, a plaque on the bridge said, passed by in 1673; an Indian massacre in 1812 right there in front of the Burger King; and vague notions of Abe Lincoln's debt to the *Chicago Tribune*, whose quaint Gothic tower looms over the bridge's north side. As any journalist knows, three instances is enough to establish a story, if not an actual trend, so I thought that's enough American history, and I could just make up the rest.

It turns out my theory was only too right. The intersection of Michigan and Wacker, I found out, isn't just a corner, it's a vortex. The deeper I dug into the history of Chicago and its relationship to the history of the country, the more crowded the ghost traffic jam clogging up the Michigan Avenue Bridge got.

The beaux arts–style bridge was constructed in 1920. Standing on it, the Chicago River flows underneath. Looking east, it isn't far from where the river meets Lake Michigan. (The river used to flow into the lake, but in 1900, engineers reversed its flow to keep the city's sewage from being deposited into its drinking water. Now the sewage eventually flows into the Mississippi, which is appreciated in Chicago, but met with less enthusiasm downriver in St. Louis.) Looking south, the bridge hits land at the corner of Michigan Avenue and Wacker Drive, where Chicagoans may purchase chocolate or eyeglasses. The view to the north is picture-postcard pretty, especially at night, when the white wedding cake of the Wrigley Building glows so soft you'd swear it's candlelit. Supposedly pictures of the building so delighted Joseph Stalin that the University of Moscow was designed in its image. And who can blame him, at least for that? In short, a 360-degree glance from the bridge offers the most dignified panorama in all Chicago. But under the Wacker Drive sidewalk, there's some very old blood seeping into the river.

The American national mythology revolves around the idea that the promise of America is best seen in the West—wide open spaces, don't fence me in, home, home on the range, etc. Metaphorically, that might be true. But economically, the real place to witness the promise of America is the Midwest, where, for most of this country's history, the products of the range were manipulated for fun and profit. When the cowboys serenaded their stray calves to "Git Along, Little Dogies," they left out the part where the little dogie is railroaded to Chicago to be slaughtered by some underpaid, overworked immigrant, en route to its manifest destiny as a New Yorker's supper.

The first person to grasp the significance of this place where the Chicago River meets Lake Michigan was Louis Joliet. Joliet was a twenty-seven-year-old fur trader who accompanied a Jesuit missionary named Jacques Marquette on a canoe expedition from Quebec in 1673. They were to map the Mississippi in the name of France, unaware that Spain had already claimed the river some 130 years before. On the return trip, at the suggestion of their Indian guide, they traveled from the Mississippi into the Illinois River, and then the Des Plaines. They got out and carried their canoes a few dozen miles to the Chicago River, where they got back in their canoes and paddled to this spot where the river meets the Great Lake—just below the corner at Michigan and Wacker.

And Joliet then had a vision. His map of North America, an oddly pretty, delicate ink drawing he made in 1674, is concerned with one thing, and one thing only—water. His America is all Great Lakes and Mississippi. Look close and you can see what he saw: From Lake Michigan, there is only one point—the future site of Chicago—that connects to a river that connects to a couple of other rivers that could connect it to the Mississippi. This is what Joliet knew, that this place is a continental hub, the missing link between the Great Lakes and the Mississippi, and

thus the Atlantic and the Gulf. All that was needed was a short canal
spanning the miles of prairie between rivers. He wrote, "We could go
with facility to Florida in a bark, and by very easy navigation." Thus
Joliet's map isn't so much a map as a prophecy: Stick your ear up against
it and you can practically hear cash registers ring.

I like to picture Joliet sometimes, walking up or down Michigan Avenue to the bridge, a go-cup in his hand from either the Starbucks on
the south side of the bridge or the Starbucks on the north side, spitting
coffee-laced saliva into the Chicago River, knowing it'll float—with facility—all the way past New Orleans and to the ocean from there.

The first person to get cracking on Joliet's dream was Chicago's
first permanent settler, Jean Baptiste Point du Sable, a trader who
moved to the north side of the river in 1779. That was in the middle of
the American Revolution, and a century after Joliet paddled by. Du
Sable's mother was an African slave and his father was French. He
was born in the Caribbean, on the island of Hispaniola. Which connects the land around the Michigan Avenue Bridge all the way back to
Columbus. Hispaniola, much to the dismay of its inhabitants, happened to be the place where Christopher Columbus dropped off forty
of his Spanish raper/pillagers on Christmas Eve 1492 as he headed
back for Spain, where he reported that the people he called Indians
"had very good faces" but "could all be subjugated and compelled to
do anything one wishes." Of course, certain settlers at Michigan and
Wacker who met death by tomahawk in 1812 might have begged to dif-
fer with that assessment.

Du Sable built a small wood cabin on what is now the site of a thirty-five-story office tower called the Equitable Building. With his Potawatomi wife, Catherine, du Sable's marriage bed was itself a map of America—the mixing of European, African, and Indian blood to make a son and a daughter, true American children with three continents in their dark eyes.

Chicago schoolteachers like to impress upon their students that Chicago's first resident, du Sable, was a black man. And just think, it only took 204 years for the town to elect its first black mayor.

The United States declared war on Great Britain in June of 1812, partly because of boundary issues here in the Old Northwest, though the news didn't reach Fort Dearborn until mid-July. Just as the soldiers and their families were evacuating the fort on August 15, hundreds of Potawatomi Indians descended upon them and killed them, burning down the fort. Today, the site of the fort is weirdly commemorated with little bronze markers embedded in the sidewalk at Michigan and Wacker, so that the tourists may dance around its former perimeter as if learning to cha-cha-cha. A wildly racist relief sculpture on the southeast corner of the bridge depicts the defense of Fort Dearborn. A soldier from the fort is battling off a savage Indian brave while a mother and child are cowering behind him, basically waiting to die. And underneath that is a plaque that says the people of the fort "were brutally massacred by the Indians. They will be cherished as martyrs in our early history." What it doesn't say is that those Indians had not technically ceded their rights to this land and they were allied with the British in a war declared by the United States, but it looks like the city ran out of room to put that on the plaque. When soldiers arrived to rebuild the fort, they first had to bury the scalped human remains, which still lay there.

Walking back onto the bridge, if you look downriver a few blocks west, you can see the site of the old Sauganash Hotel. During the first half of the nineteenth century, at the Sauganash, Chicagoans seemed to be playacting the juiciest bits of the country's spanking-new Constitution every night. In his book *City of the Century*, historian Donald L. Miller writes: "At the Sauganash and its neighboring hotels, men and women of every color and class were welcome; and whiskey, song, and dance were the great democratizers. Visitors from more civilized parts were shocked to see Indian braves spinning the white wives of fort officers around the dance floor of the Sauganash to the frenzied fiddling and toe tapping of [hotel owner] Mark Beaubien, or Indian and white women drinking home-distilled liquor straight from the bottle. To add an edge to the evenings, local white traders . . . would put on feathered headdresses and spring into the crowded tavern with war whoops and raised tomahawks, scaring the wits out of tight-buttoned easterners."

Could there be a more lovable historical yarn than that? That anecdote is endearing, not just as a metaphor for the best American ideals—the picture of liquored-up ladies and dancing Indians, the strangeness of reenacting the Fort Dearborn massacre to scare the queasy Easterners, turning what must have still been an open wound

into a practical joke. That story is proof of the theorem that then as today in Chicago, the mysterious equation of whiskey plus music equals
what can only be called happiness.

The festivities were brief. The ladies of Chicago wouldn't be dancing with Indians much longer because there wouldn't be any Indians
left to dance with. The City of Chicago was officially incorporated in
1833, the year the Potawatomi chiefs stood near the site where the Equitable Building stands today and signed away their land in Illinois to
the administration of Andrew Jackson, who found time in his busy
schedule of relocating the Cherokee, Creek, Choctaw, Chickasaw, and
Seminole to have the Potawatomi removed west to what U.S. government surveyors had called land "too poor for snakes to live upon."

Three years after the Potawatomi signed away their land and the city
was incorporated, construction began on that canal that Joliet had en-
visioned a century and a half before, to connect Lake Michigan to the
Mississippi. The Illinois and Michigan Canal took twelve years to
build, dug almost entirely by hand, mostly by Irish immigrants, who
crossed an ocean and the prairie for the privilege of keeling over with a
shovel in their hands. They did not die in vain. The canal worked
pretty much exactly as Joliet imagined. So much trade moved past this
corner that Chicago expanded from a muddy little hamlet of a few
hundred people to city of over a hundred thousand in just twenty-five
years.

Thanks in part to one particular innovation born next to the Michigan Avenue Bridge, Chicago was not the only city in America to ex-

perience a population boom in the last half of the nineteenth century. Cyrus McCormick built his McCormick Reaper Works right here on the river in 1847. His machine, the reaper, turned out to be one of the most significant inventions in the history of history. Before Mc-Cormick it took three hours to gather a bushel of wheat, and with the reaper it took ten minutes.

Because McCormick helped mechanize agriculture, farms could use less labor in less time and produce more crops on more land. By speeding up and emptying out the country, McCormick populated the city. Not that the march of progress is necessarily benign, especially if you're one of those urban workers—just ask the dead of the Haymarket riot who laid down their lives just fifteen blocks from here for the eight-hour workday, or read Upton Sinclair's *The Jungle* about what the meatpackers went through on the South Side, or listen to the words of Cyrus McCormick himself, who, along with merchant Marshall Field, secretly bought Gatling guns for the Illinois National Guard in case of "what danger, if any, was to be anticipated from the communistic element of the city."

By the Civil War, most of America's grain from the West and the vast prairie around Chicago was unloaded from trains here, traded on the commodities exchange, and then sent east on ships from Lake Michigan, all within a five-minute walk of the corner of Michigan Avenue and Wacker Drive. It could have been this very spot the poet Carl Sandburg was thinking of in his famous poem "Chicago." He called the city "Tool Maker, Stacker of Wheat, Player with Railroads and the Nation's Freight Handler; Stormy, husky, brawling, City of the Big Shoulders." The reaper works on the north side of the river was the Tool Maker. The Stacker of Wheat was in the giant grain silos on the south side of the river where the giant Hyatt Hotel stands. The Player with Railroads and the Nation's Freight Handler was over on the train tracks next to the silos. And you can spot the big shoulders attached to roughly nine out of ten men walking by.

It is my project to tell the whole history of America from this corner, and there's no telling of that history without the Civil War. Abraham Lincoln was nominated for president here in Chicago at the Republican National Convention in 1860, on the very site, by the way, of the old Sauganash Hotel where the Indians and drunken ladies used to dance.

And the Chicago Tribune Tower, standing on North Michigan Avenue a stone's throw from the bridge, not only campaigned for Lincoln, its editors talked him into running for president in the first place. Lincoln was considering going for vice president. Maybe.

As a subscriber who reads the *Trib* every morning, it is difficult for me to get all misty-eyed with idealism over the paper's current state. Let's just say I identified with the guy I saw not long ago on Michigan Avenue, at the height of the Age of Lewinsky, grab a *Tribune* vending machine and wrest it from its moorings in the sidewalk, slamming it to the ground. But the *Tribune*'s heroic past is another story. Every time I'm about to cancel my subscription just to save myself from recycling, I remember that Abe Lincoln subscribed, and throw yet another fat Sunday edition on top of the little *Tribune* tower in my apartment.

The *Trib*'s great editor Joseph Medill helped found the Republican Party to advance the antislavery cause. Medill was such a passionate abolitionist that he wrote in a *Tribune* editorial in 1856, "We are not unfrequently told that we crowd the *Tribune* with antislavery matter to the exclusion of other topics . . . we plead guilty."

Medill and company's friendship with the president wasn't necessarily always in their favor. At the height of the Civil War, they went to the White House and pleaded to get out of the president's new request for six thousand more Union draftees from Cook County and Chicago—this after the area had already given up some twenty-two thousand men. According to writer Lloyd Wendt, after Medill asked for mercy, Lincoln turned on him with that Lincolnesque biblical wrath, scolding, "It is you who are largely responsible for making blood flow as it has. You called for war until we had it. You called for Emancipation, and I have given it to you. Whatever you have asked you have had. Now you come here begging to be let off from the call for men which I have made to carry out the war you have demanded. You ought to be ashamed of yourselves. I have a right to expect better things of you. Go home, and raise your six thousand extra men."

Needless to say, Lincoln got his Chicago soldiers. And, reporting the news of the president's assassination on April 15, 1865, the headline of the *Chicago Tribune* simply reads, "Terrible News."

The whole city burned to the ground, in the Great Chicago Fire of 1871, and the city became the place where every major architect in the country, from Louis Sullivan and Frank Lloyd Wright on down to Mies van der Rohe, worked on reinventing what a city skyline is supposed to look like. Montgomery Ward—just a few blocks down Michigan from the bridge—and Sears and Roebuck revolutionized consumer merchandising, with mail-order catalog sales. In 1920, Al Capone came to town, the same year Prohibition went into effect. One year after that, Vincent "The Schemer" Drucci, a member of the Dion O'Banion gang, chased by police, drove onto the Michigan Avenue Bridge just as it was opening to let a boat pass. He jumped the gap, only to crash straight into the other side.

Decades pass. Manufacturing at the corner gives way to the service economy—now it's all banks and advertising agencies and law firms, skyscrapers instead of warehouses. Railroads give way to the world's busiest airport, on the north side of town. Only an eight-minute walk from the corner is the site of the first Kennedy-Nixon debate, the place, you could argue, where modern televised democracy begins, since that's the debate Nixon was said to lose not because of the issues but because he looked so ghastly sweating under the lights. And just a short walk from there is the building where Hugh Hefner ran *Playboy* magazine during its heyday.

As long as we're on the subject of the decline of Western civilization, the second floor of the NBC Tower, tucked between the Equitable Building and the Tribune Tower, is where *The Jerry Springer Show* is taped. It just wouldn't be the haunted landscape around the Michigan Avenue Bridge if some symbolic television apocalypse did not happen here each day. The constant profanity makes the show into an unintelligible barrage of bleeps. Watching it is like listening to a constant storm warning, which is exactly what it is.

Maybe it's just a coincidence, but one way you can measure the importance of this corner to our national psyche is the number of times it shows up in motion pictures—specifically, the action-adventure kind. Bruce Willis, Samuel L. Jackson, Kevin Costner, Sean Connery, Tommy Lee Jones, Wesley Snipes, Harrison Ford, Kevin Spacey—there's barely an actor worth the cover of *Entertainment Weekly* who hasn't been in a film with a scene shot right at the corner. And why? Because these films are about the motion of planes, trains, automobiles, boats, helicopters, motorcycles—every modern means of transportation. And so where better to film them than the place that three centuries ago was spotted as our country's leading transportation hub by Hollywood's favorite unintentional location scout: Louis Joliet.

In one typical offering, *Chain Reaction*, Keanu Reeves plays a fugitive motorcycle-riding University of Chicago machinist being framed for murder, treason, and terrorism. Being framed is usually a big part of all these movies. Attempting to elude the police, he's chased down Michigan Avenue to the Michigan Avenue Bridge. The bridge starts opening, and Keanu scurries up, a cop not far behind. He does a little better than Vincent "The Schemer" Drucci did in the '20s, but then, Keanu's a movie star, has a stunt double, and can do retakes. As the angle of the raised bridge gets steeper, the cop slides to the bottom. Keanu's at the top. What should he do? He looks up—a police helicopter. He looks down—a police boat. He crawls into the bottom of the bridge as it's lowered and ducks into a garbage truck to safety. When he meets his fellow, shapely fugitive, who nervously awaits him at the train station, the conductor asks, "What took you so long?" To which Keanu deadpans, "The bridge was up."

Up, down, north, south—whatever. The point is that the bridge was. Right at the center of attention, in the middle of the action, at the hub. We used to ship grain from this corner. Now that entertainment is America's second biggest export, the product we ship is Keanu.

Species-on-Species Abuse

I AM STANDING ON DISNEY WORLD'S MAIN STREET, U.S.A., WATCHING CIN-
derella go by. I am watching, but the three-year-old next to me plays
with a knob on his stroller. His grandparents, or at least I assume
they're his grandparents, are sweating and waving their arms and
wearing panicked smiles trying to get his attention, pointing at Cinderella and then the Little Mermaid, yelling, Look! Look!, their eyes
full of melting dollar signs, wondering why oh why they came all this
way and shelled out so many Disney Dollars to fly here and stay here
and be here just so the little fellow could obsess over a plastic bump—a
beige plastic bump—on his goddamn stroller. After a few minutes,
Grandma gives up and, I'm pretty sure, vows to amend her will.

Me, I'm with the kid on this. So is my friend David, who, as Cinderella's procession passes, tells me, "Look at all the communications
majors!" There is better stuff to stare at in the Magic Kingdom than

coeds dressed up like cartoon characters. The sadly underrated life-size animatronic Lyndon Johnson, for example.

David and I came to Disney World for the same reasons everyone comes to Disney World: to reaffirm our faith in the U.S. Constitution, contemplate the profound influence of the American presidency on our lives, and revisit the literary legacy of Mark Twain. Well, that's not true. We came to Disney World because we had nonrefundable plane tickets to Orlando to see a NASA shuttle launch at the Kennedy Space Center and when that got scrubbed, we figured, what the hell, Disney.

Neither of us has ever been to a Disney anything before, except of course for the movies. I lived in Oklahoma as a child. My family never went to Disney World or Disneyland for the same reason we never went to either coast. My parents' U.S.A. is a triangle of the continent fenced in between Butte, Santa Fe, and Little Rock. So my childhood theme park was Dogpatch, a hillbilly wonderland in Arkansas with banjo players, faux run-down shacks, and ample goat-petting opportunities. There are a lot of pictures of my sister and me with our arms around cartoonish mountain folk with corncob pipes clenched between their blackened teeth who bore an unsettling resemblance to our own grandparents.

It isn't that difficult to talk a boy into going all the way to Florida to watch a rocket launch, even a gay, Jewish Canadian resident of Manhattan like David. Coaxing him into Disney World was another story. When I inform him that the shuttle launch has been postponed and

broach the subject of Disney World instead, his first reaction is horror. He talks himself into it as a scientific experiment. He sounds like
an ambivalent med student about to dissect a corpse when he theo-
rizes, "Disney World is like the liver of the country where the blood of
America gets filtered."

"I'm going to take that as a yes," I answer, and book a hotel room.

The Magic Kingdom, which opened in 1971, is the oldest section of
Disney World. We walk through the famous Cinderella castle, which
I've seen so many thousands of times on the opening credits of television's *Wonderful World of Disney*, and I find myself looking up into the
sky for Tinkerbell to twitter by. We're on our way to the patriotic
neighborhood called Liberty Square.

Supposedly, other childless adults do vacation at Disney World.
Though when I met him at the Orlando airport, David informed me
that because of all the screaming kids on his flight he could make a
fortune setting up a tubal ligation and vasectomy clinic at the gate. The
obvious reason for childless adults to visit Disney World is to recap-
ture a bit of their youth. Which is precisely what I'm doing as I pull
David into the Hall of Presidents. Nobody said everyone's youth was
fun! fun! fun! Aside from the occasional Dogpatch outing, my childhood tourist experiences were mostly of the semi-grisly edutainment
variety: Boot Hill, Civil War battlefields, the site of Custer's Last Stand.
I have no roller-coaster nostalgia whatsoever, though I do sometimes
pine for getting my picture taken next to old tombstones and Confederate cannons and sitting in dark, air-conditioned rooms watching

film strips with stiff narrators coughing up a bunch of dates and casualty statistics and phrases like "brother against brother."

Hence the Hall of Presidents, a theater resembling a Federalist Vegas lounge. David deems the wainscoting appropriately sober, but sizes up the shimmering textiles in front of us by exclaiming, "Those curtains arc *fabulous.*" An authoritative voice warns against flash photography "in order to preserve the dignity of the presentation." But that doesn't inspire the man behind us to remove his mouse ears. The lights go down and the fabulous curtain goes up and "Dr." Maya Angelou, the original Goofy, narrates a brief film highlighting American history from the Declaration of Independence through the space age. Angelou's voice is so irregular, so bumpy, she might be skateboarding down a cobblestone street. She jiggles around syllables so that the first phrase of the Constitution comes off as "We the peephole." Which is unintentionally accurate, now if not then, when one takes into account the rise of voyeurism, surveillance, and princess-killing tabloids. The film lacks a certain razzle-dazzle. I thought Disney was all about showbiz, but the dramaturge of this spectacle is so wrapped up in the tension between the central government and states' rights that it features a weirdly longish segment on South Carolina and nullification. I haven't heard the word "nullification" spoken out loud since eleventh-grade AP American history with Mr. Corne. What's next? Ladies and gentlemen, the Occupational Safety and Health Act of 1970! Disney's decision to include like three whole minutes on the debate over whether South Carolina, and therefore everyone else, could nullify bits of the Constitution à la carte is a sort of subtle choice, but Angelou's lionization of anti-nullification president Andrew Jackson as "brilliant, roughhewn, and courageous" makes sense considering there would be no Disney World at all if Jackson had not stolen away the very land we're sitting on from the Seminole tribe. But I digress.

The Lincoln segment is the best. (Isn't it always?) It features imposing music and pictures of the president brooding over the impending, according to Angelou, "bit-tah and blood-eeeeee wa-ar." We hear the "house divided" speech, watch as slavery is outlawed and the Union is preserved. After that, it's a quick clip from the golden spike to a rocket blasting off. Then—surprise!—the curtain rises to reveal all forty-two American presidents, or at least their audio-animatronic likenesses. They're all here—every last wig-wearing, waistcoat-sporting chief, every familiar face and forgotten bureaucrat from Washington to Clinton, who, according to my guidebook, recorded his voice especially for this presentation. The presidents are a little creepy, not quite real but not quite dead, just not quite right. I swear the Reagan is *looking at me.* Then, like some kind of presidential graduation day, the name of each man is called and a light shines on his face. Lincoln's name is greeted with a big "Woooooo!" from the back of the hall, as if he were the captain of the football team. When it's Chester A. Arthur's moment in the spotlight, my green card–carrying Canadian companion whispers, "I've literally never heard of him." When the list ends at the current president, Bill Clinton spouts the kind of Americana rhetoric he's so good at, words that I fell for back in his first presidential campaign—words that I'm falling for now. When he says, "Let us pause to honor the very idea of America," he has me. I'm a sucker for such talk, and so what? "There is nothing wrong with America that cannot be cured by what is right with America." He might even mean it, and what's more, I might even believe it. By the time the fabulous curtain comes down, to the strains of the "Battle Hymn of the Republic" thank you very much, I am wiping a tear from my eye and David has his hand over his heart.

Boy, all that glory glory hallelujah sure makes you hungry. We exit the theater and agree that it is time to "Liberate Your Appetite" with a late lunch at the Liberty Tree Tavern, a re-created eighteenth-century pub complete with fireplace, plank flooring, pewter, and realistically blurry windows of hand-pressed glass. It is staffed by servers in traditional period costumes, costumes which come to a screeching halt at the footwear, unless black Reebok high-tops were on the market in 1776.

The maître d' announces customers as if they're representatives to the Continental Congress, barking their last names and that of their home state. He gives a bell to a small child from "the Great State of Pennsylvania" who is supposed to ring in the meal. The child yells a phrase the maître d' whispered into his ear: "Hairy! Hairy! Hairy!" Probably he's supposed to say "Here Ye," but I'm not one to knock the healing power of childhood Disney mispronunciation: When I was four, my parents made an appointment with an ear, nose, and throat specialist the moment they realized I was half deaf, rendering the

Mickey Mouse Club theme lyric "Forever let us hold our banner high" as "For every little polar bear to hide."

"The Vowell Family from the Great State of Illinois" is seated and served the Patriot's Platter—a family-style Thanksgiving dinner. I'm not quite sure if I feel particularly patriotic about strawberry vinaigrette on my Declaration Salad, though I gladly pledge allegiance to the mashed potatoes of the United States of America. We order Cokes because there's no ale in the pub. Magic Kingdom is dry for the kiddies' sake, though one wonders if Sam Adams's generation would have fought so hard to build a democratic nation with such despotic liquor laws.

It is a dizzying meal in that its Disneyness lurches in and out of focus. David and I talk about whatever it is we always talk about—our shared affinity for Warren Beatty's *Reds*, his idea for a support group he wants to start called Adult Children of Parents. But every few minutes, one of the poor bastards dressed up as a Disney character saunters over to our table to interact. Some of the other adults in the room are really good at this—videotaping, pretending to tickle Chip (or is it Dale?), joshing around with Minnie Mouse. As Minnie approaches our table, I quickly finish my sentence, a sentence ending in the word "bereft." In order to ward off the characters, David suggests that every time one of them comes over one of us should stage whisper, "Are you saying nobody's ever given you the clap before?" But mostly we just freeze in speechless horror every time one of them stops by. Unbeknownst to David, who is going on about his alma mater Columbia

University, Goofy is standing behind him flashing the victory sign over his head and I'm in stitches. When David finally notices Goofy, he admits, "I was wondering why the General Studies program was getting such a laugh."

We march out of the ersatz Philadelphia of Liberty Square into the ersatz Wild West called Frontierland. We stop off in the Frontierland Shootin' Arcade. David, one of my all-time favorite sissies, has a cabinet in his Manhattan apartment which he refers to as the "craft cupboard" when he isn't calling it the "art supplies armoire." Nevertheless, here he is in Frontierland squinting at a fake fur gopher through the scope of an air rifle and ruggedly pulling the trigger. It must be something he picked up on the wild frontier of downtown Toronto. If the shootin' comes naturally to him, he cannot get over Frontierland's favorite snack—Henry VIII–sized roasted turkey legs. These gigantoid drumsticks are being consumed as if they were the most normal fast food on earth, like pretzels or hot dogs. No one is asking anyone, "Hey! Get a picture of me with a giant turkey leg!" But then we notice a family throwing scraps of turkey leg at some pigeons, i.e., feeding birds bird, which David deems "species-on-species abuse."

Aside from the ornithological cannibalism and the Cinderella parade which David refers to as "a relentless mocking of my purported sanity," we're pleasantly surprised at how tasteful the Magic Kingdom is. There aren't that many movie tie-ins. In fact, as we make our way to Tom Sawyer Island, it seems like the only tie-in is Mark Twain.

I cherish the memory of the autumn of my sixth-grade year in which, every afternoon, our class got to sit on the floor and listen to our teacher offer chapters of Tom and Huck and Becky and that awful Injun Joe. It is magnanimous, if not bad for business, for a motion picture and television empire like Disney to devote Disney World space to the promotion of literature. Doesn't Disney lose money every time a child cracks open a book?

I am drawn to Tom Sawyer Island because a tribute to Mark Twain would not be out of place in a theme park of my own design. Should Vowell World ever get enough investors, I'm going to stick my Tom Sawyer Island in Love and Death in the American Novel Land right between the Jay Gatsby Swimming Pool and Tom Joad's Dust Bowl Lanes, a Depression-themed bowling alley renting artfully worn-out shoes.

To set foot on Tom Sawyer Island, one must board a raft à la Huck and Jim. Floating to shore reminds me of my favorite paragraph of *Huckleberry Finn*, the plain poetry of the way Huck narrates, "It's lovely to live on a raft. We had the sky up there, all speckled with stars, and we used to lay on our backs and look up at them, and discuss about whether they was made or only just happened." David, my own huckleberry friend, has similarly Twainlike talents as a naturalist, describing the rustic island as "just like the Ramble at Central Park, but without the men jerking each other off."

The best thing on the island is Injun Joe's Cave. A sign at its entrance reads, "Do not wurry. Injun Joe ain't been seen in thess parts for a long time. His cave is deeserted!" As a sixth grader I was, right alongside Tom and Huck, terrified of the murderer Injun Joe. I know that the dark, cramped, and deeserted cave is making David as nervous as I am when he reassures me, "I've got Xanax!" We are relieved to reach the exit, marked up with edgier material than the "Tom + Becky" whitewash graffiti outside: "Fuck Off Nazis" is scrawled on the wall.

We then follow a map to Indian Territory. It's obviously a reference to the final two sentences of *Huckleberry Finn* in which Huck says, "I reckon I got to light out for the territory ahead of the rest, because Aunt Sally she's going to adopt me and sivilize me, and I can't stand it. I been there before." But when we arrive at the territory, we scratch our heads, wondering what it means that the territory is blocked off. The emblem of freedom is literally a dead end. Did the Disney planners just plunk the territory here at the edge because they were running out of room and that's where the book ends? Or is the Magic Kingdom offering some sophisticated commentary on the elusive nature of the American dream? And then again, by restricting access to the promised land, is Disney telling us that the important thing is lighting out, that the journey matters more than the destination? Standing here mulling over such questions is itself a kind of ride, and the lines aren't as long as they are at Splash Mountain.

I'm a meaning junkie anyway, but lately, the whole country's on symbolism alert. Huck and Tom are the archetypical American boys, and American boys are this year's pariahs. We're walking around Tom Sawyer Island exactly one month after two teenage boys in Littleton,

Colorado, opened fire on their classmates at Columbine High. Talk about species-on-species abuse. The boys killed twelve students, one teacher, and then killed themselves. I'm taken aback at how much that event colors the world, colors Disney World. All the kids I bump into and step on—here they're so plentiful and so short I have to say "I'm sorry" every thirty seconds—seem less like real children and more like Symbols of Childhood.

Before I came here I asked my friend Sara, the best-read twelve-year-old I know, if she had read *The Adventures of Tom Sawyer* and she had not. Unlike a lot of old-fashioned children's books—the Hardy Boys series, *Little Women*—*Tom Sawyer* and *Huckleberry Finn* might be less universally read not because they're so tame but because they're not tame enough. Even I can understand why teachers might shy away from Tom's rambunctious antics—the pirate fantasies, running away, sassing your aunt, tricking others to paint the fence you've been assigned. Huck even *smokes.* Add to that the liberal usage of a certain synonym for the term "African American" and the fact that the villain is half Indian (and, groan, named Injun), and I can see how the book wouldn't fit into the treacly "values" units that are the educational vogue. I wonder how the teachers who were doing *Huckleberry Finn* the week of Littleton handled the joking beginning, in which Tom starts his own gang and informs Huck and the other boys that their reason for being is "nothing but robbery and murder." Children's books can't say that anymore, even in jest. Which is too bad, because even though the two books' boy-talk brags about killing, when Tom and Huck witness an actual murder it terrifies them, and Injun Joe the murderer is the object of their disgust and fear. *Tom Sawyer* articulates the difference between the language of child's play and the consequences of evil.

The next morning David and I are watching CNN in Disney's Contemporary Resort as we pack and they cut to breaking news: A kid in Conyers, Georgia, just opened fire at his school, wounding six fellow students. The shooter is fifteen years old.

We still have a day to kill. I wouldn't mind sticking around Disney World and going on some rides. But yesterday in Frontierland, when I asked David if he would accompany me on a roller coaster that winds through an abandoned mine shaft, he recoiled as though I'd just asked him to French-kiss a girl. So we've agreed to spend our last hours in Florida visiting the Disney-planned community next to Disney World called Celebration, a town that might be described as Life: The Ride. It's a sort of Main Street, U.S.A., in three dimensions.

If ever there were a town constructed for the purpose of making kids feel safe, it's Celebration. As a cab drives us past the perfect houses to the center of town, I can't help but wonder if I would have looked at these eerily charming porches differently two months ago (before Littleton and the new shooting this morning, but long enough after all the other school shootings last year for the child murderer memories to fade a little). I might have laughed off Celebration's purposeful wholesomeness as parental paranoia. But after four straight weeks of teenage bullet wounds and funeral footage, I cannot dismiss the impulse to circle the wagons here in Our Town.

Still, in post-Watergate, post-Vietnam America, odds are that the more you shoot for Frank Capra, the more likely you are to end up with David Lynch. Once I notice that the town diner where we're having breakfast is about to celebrate something as corny as National Chocolate Ice Cream Day I start looking for lopped-off earlobes in my hash browns.

Established by Disney in 1994, Celebration's planners have tried hard to answer some of the criticism of suburbs—that the houses are all alike, that there aren't any sidewalks, that they're organized around automobiles. While nearly every house on each block has a porch to encourage neighborly socialization, stylistically, each house is different: a clapboard next to stucco around the corner from a cute Cape Cod. According to an official architectural walking-tour booklet, "The town places special emphasis on restoring streets and sidewalks to the public realm on the assumption that streets should belong to people, not cars."

We rent bikes and ride them to the real estate office, where we watch a soft-focus promotional film for the town in which earnest parents talk up the pleasures of living in a place where "everybody has the same ideals." A nullification of the First Amendment? Maybe Celebration succeeded where South Carolina failed. Well, the joke's on them. Sometime, and sometime soon, all those adorable towheaded kids in the promotional film are going to turn thirteen. Once a family member hits puberty, odds are that everybody is not going to have the same ideals. Unless everybody gets together and agrees that the new ideals involve turning the front yard into a skate ramp and officially changing Dad's name to Fuckhead.

As Huck Finn might put it, this town sure is sivilized. And since every teenager worth the word has a little Huck in her, Celebration is almost the perfect place to be *from*, to light out from—the perfect place to leave. Even though—maybe because—Celebration is meant to be a symbol of stability, it appears so fragile. Perhaps it's all that fresh paint. The town looks too clean, too new, too perfect to hold up. It's just standing there, immaculate, waiting to be violated, waiting for the paint to chip or a drought to dry up the lawns, waiting for the patina of age and decay. If its greatest purpose is to be an upstanding environment in which to raise children, it resembles a child—no wrinkles, soft skin, soft hair. It doesn't look like a place for real men and women to live real life.

We ride our bikes past the kind of views that have become rare in the messier, less intentionally constructed parts of the country. We turn onto a bike path bordering a wetlands preserve, and out of my right eye I can see herons, wild turkeys, turtles, and a thick brushy primeval forest that probably hasn't changed since Osceola himself left Osceola County. My left eye ogles a row of immaculate houses and rectangular, Crayola green lawns. It is a split screen of nature and culture, the pre-Columbian and the oh so post-. Even though the houses are surely infringing on the wetlands, it looks like that jungle will return to claim its own, swallowing the superfluous buildings whole.

David, alluding to the last page of *The Great Gatsby*, nods at the wetlands and says, "Look! It's the fresh, green breast of the new world!" It is the most beautiful passage ever written about the promise of America. In it, Nick, a Midwesterner, stands on what had been Gatsby's lawn looking across Long Island Sound and muses, "And as the moon rose higher the inessential houses began to melt away until gradually I became aware of the old island here that flowered once for Dutch sailors' eyes—a fresh, green breast of the new world. Its vanished trees, the trees that had made way for Gatsby's house, had once pandered in whispers to the last and greatest of all human dreams; for a transitory enchanted moment man must have held his breath in the presence of this continent, compelled into an aesthetic contemplation he neither understood nor desired, face to face for the last time in history with something commensurate to his capacity for wonder."

I adore those words, worship them actually, and yet I do not buy that part about "the last time in history." Because the narrator himself is having such a wondrous moment; because every American who comes to love this lovable, hateful place knows this wonder, too. Because screeching the brakes on my rental bike and watching a turtle that is who knows how old creep across the wilderness of palm fronds that juts against such a painfully cute subset of civilization, I know exactly why the painfully cute civilization wants to be here, build here, make their homes and babies at such a place. So what if they got it wrong? Is there anything more American than constructing some squeaky-clean city on a hill looking out across the terrible beauty of this land? While most of the rest of us have internalized these impulses, turned them into metaphors, at Celebration, Disney is attempting the real deal; like the Puritans and the pioneers, they're carving out a new community.

An eerie, xenophobic, nostalgic community I can't wait to leave, but still.

David, poor thing, is about to drop dead of heat stroke. He tells me, "It *looks* like a Norman Rockwell town, but it's so hot he'd have to paint everybody with enormously enlarged pores." And if he were not drenched enough already, he starts tearing up in the cab to the airport as the elderly driver tells us the story about how her perfect life degenerated when her husband had a stroke and she lost her business and now has to drive a cab and live with an aunt. Her story isn't making David cry—her Disneylike cheerfulness is. When she drops us off she smiles and chirps, "You've got to come back and stay longer!" David gives her an ungodly tip and reassures her that we'd love to, though once she drives away he mutters, "No. We will never come back."

OBITUARIES

What I See When I Look at the Face on the $20 Bill

BEING AT LEAST A LITTLE CHEROKEE IN EASTERN OKLAHOMA WHERE I WAS born is about as rare and remarkable as being a Michael Jordan fan in Chicago. I mean, who isn't? Both my parents are Cherokee to varying degrees, and I'm between an eighth and a quarter. It goes without saying that my twin sister, Amy, is, too. Except that I have dark eyes and dark hair and she's a blue-eyed blond, and so our grandfather nicknamed me Injun and her Swede.

"Those roles were assigned to us, Indian and Swede," Amy says, "because of the way we looked. But it was also more like the things we were told about ourselves." She mentions that when we were children, I was the one given the Cherokee language book and she was told she resembled our Swedish grandmother who died before we were born. She continues, "I think I was probably six or seven before I realized that I was Cherokee, too."

We're a little French and Scottish and English and Seminole, too, typical American mutts. But the Cherokee and Swedish sides of the family were the only genealogies anyone in the family knew anything about. Here's what we knew about ourselves: Ellis Island, Trail of Tears. And I think, to a kid, "Trail of Tears," the Cherokees' forced march from the East to Oklahoma where we were born, seemed enormously more interesting, just as a name. Even the smallest children know what tears mean, and I think in my earliest understanding of where I came from, I pictured myself descended from a long line of weepers with bloodshot eyes. The Trail of Tears took place in 1838–39, when the U.S. Army wrenched sixteen thousand people from their homes in Georgia, North Carolina, and Tennessee, rounded them up in stockades, and marched them away, across hundreds of miles. Four thousand died.

Every summer when we were children, our parents would drive us to a place about half an hour from where we lived called Tsa-La-Gi, which is the Cherokee word for Cherokee. It's the tribe's cultural center. There's a re-created precolonial village, a museum, and—this was our favorite part—an amphitheater which staged a dramatic re-creation of the Trail of Tears. Every summer we watched Chief John Ross try like mad to save the Cherokee land back east. We saw his hot-head rival Stand Watie rage off to the Civil War. We especially loved the Death of the Phoenix, a noisy, magenta-lit interpretive dance in which the mythic bird would die only to rise again.

Amy took it to heart: "The play was really tragic. I have a reverent feeling toward it. And I think it's because this play was so serious and told such a detailed story that it took this place of significance. It was really important. It really mattered."

The amphitheater show so influenced my thinking that even though my dad and my grandfather used to show me photographs of Cherokee leaders like Stand Watie in books, when I imagine Stand Watie now I still picture the actor at Tsa-La-Gi.

So all my life I knew I wouldn't exist but for the Trail of Tears, and it struck me as a little silly that most of the things I knew about it were based on an amphitheater drama I haven't seen for twenty years. I had read some books about the Trail but I wanted to see it, feel it, know how long the distance was. I wanted the trek to be real. I enlisted Amy, who, unlike me, has a license. Perhaps she'd like to do all the driving? A historical tragedy and five fourteen-hour days behind the wheel? Who could pass that up? And so I fly from Chicago, she from Montana, and one spring morning we find ourselves in a rental car on our way to northwestern Georgia, the homeland of the Cherokee before they were shoved out to Oklahoma, the place the Trail of Tears begins.

The Cherokee territory once encompassed most of present-day Tennessee and Kentucky, as well as parts of Alabama, Georgia, Virginia, and the Carolinas. Even before contact with Europeans in 1540, they were a protodemocratic society. They built these enormous council houses, big enough to fit the entire tribe inside, so everyone could participate in tribal decisions.

We're barely on the road an hour when we spot them: Injuns. Ceramic ones, three feet tall, at a shack on the side of the road. Amy drives past them, we do a double take, and we don't even discuss whether or not to stop, she just backs up immediately and parks.

"Are you of Native American descent?" I ask the proprietor.

"I'm a Mexican. I'm from Texas," he answers.

"And what brought you to Calhoun, Georgia?"

"The work."

The eight little Indians he's selling are of the kitschy, teepee-toting, Plains Indian, squaws and braves variety. Which are probably easier to sell than the stereotypical image of a Cherokee—a tired out old woman tromping through the Trail of Tears in rags. Who wants that as a lawn ornament?

"Who buys these Indian statues?" I ask.

"People here from Calhoun. People around here from Georgia love Indians."

"Well, after they got rid of them?"

He laughs and says, "That's right. That's true. You're telling the truth there."

The Cherokees, who had always taken an interest in the more useful innovations of white culture, not to mention married whites at a fairly fast clip, were always a nerdy, overachiever, bookish sort of tribe. By the early nineteenth century, they launched a series of initiatives directly imitating the new American republic. In one decade, they created a written language, started a free press, ratified a constitution, and founded a capital city.

New Echota was that capital. Now it stands in the middle of nowhere—a Georgia state park with a handful of buildings across from a golf course. It was founded in 1819. To call it the Cherokee version of Washington, D.C., is entirely applicable, given the form of government the tribe established there. For the Nation sought to emulate not just the democratic structures of the United States government by dividing into legislative, judicial, and executive branches, but the best ideals of the American republic. In 1827, they ratified a constitution based on that of the United States. Its preamble begins, "We, the Representatives of the people of the Cherokee Nation in Convention assembled, in order to establish justice, ensure tranquility, promote our common welfare, and secure to ourselves and our posterity the blessings of liberty . . ."

Unlike Washington, New Echota is cool and quiet and green. Site manager David Gomez shows us around the grounds. Amy and I are unprepared for the loveliness of the place, for its calm lushness, its fragrance. Everywhere, honeysuckle is in bloom. I tell him I like it here.

"It's nice," he agrees. "It's peaceful and the atmosphere is right for what was going on and the story that we tell here. It's a story that's sad in a lot of ways, but there were a lot of great things happening with the Cherokee Nation."

The Cherokee, along with the other Southeastern tribes who suffered removal to Oklahoma—the Chickasaw, the Creek, the Choctaw, the Seminole—are one of the so-called Five Civilized Tribes. It was in 1822 that the Cherokee hero Sequoyah developed an alphabet, inventing the sole written language of any North American tribe. Only six years later, Cherokee editor Elias Boudinot founded the *Cherokee Phoenix*, a bilingual, English-Cherokee newspaper published at New Echota. Many Cherokee, especially the large population of mixed-bloods, practiced Christianity. And, because many of these lived as "civilized" Southern gentlemen of the early nineteenth century, they owned prospering plantations, which meant they owned black slaves. More than any other Native American tribe, the Cherokees adopted the religious, cultural, and political ideals of the United States. Partly as a means of self-preservation. By becoming more like the Americans, they hoped to coexist with this new nation that was growing up around them, but they weren't allowed to. Georgia settlers wanted their land. And their gold, which was discovered near New Echota in 1829.

Gomez says, "They were really progressing so fast at this time period. The printing operation was going with their newspaper here. Things were moving so fast for them for a short while here that it looked very promising, but because of the gold and the big demand for land, their fate had really been already sealed for them in earlier years."

The tribe allowed Christian missionaries to live and work among them, and to teach their children English. The most beloved of these was the Presbyterian Samuel Worcester, who built a two-story house at New Echota, which functioned as a post office, school, and rooming house. It still stands, and David Gomez walks us through, warning us of the steep steps: "You wouldn't want to have a broken leg on the rest of your trail."

The state of Georgia, which of all the Southern states treated the Cherokee with the most hostility, passed a number of alarming laws in the 1820s and '30s undermining the sovereignty of the Nation. One of these laws required white settlers within the boundaries of the Nation to obtain a permit from the state of Georgia. Samuel Worcester refused to apply for such a permit, arguing that he had the permission of the Cherokee to live on their lands and that should suffice. Georgia arrested Worcester and imprisoned him for four years. Worcester appealed to the Supreme Court, and the case, *Worcester v. Georgia*, became a great victory for the tribe. The Court, under Chief Justice John Marshall, ruled that the Cherokee Nation was just that—a sovereign nation within the borders of the U.S., and therefore beholden only to the federal government, i.e., not under the jurisdiction of Georgia state laws.

"And the Cherokee Nation was elated," Gomez points out. "They thought, 'All right, the highest court in the land of the United States—this government that we're trying to copy—they ruled in our favor. This is going to be good.' Of course, Andrew Jackson, who was pro-removal from the early years—he campaigned on that issue—decided he wasn't going to back the Supreme Court ruling."

On hearing of the ruling, the president is said to have replied, "John Marshall has made his ruling. Now let him enforce it." Think about that, what that means: a breakdown of the balance of power in such boasting, dictatorial terms. Jackson is violating his own oath of office, to uphold the Constitution. In the twentieth century, when people bandy about the idea of impeachment for presidents who fib about extramarital dalliances, it's worth remembering what a truly impeachable offense looks like. Didn't happen of course. I refer you to the face on the twenty-dollar bill.

The state of Georgia was thrilled when Jackson thumbed his nose at the Court, and immediately dispatched teams to survey the Cherokee lands for a land lottery. Soon white settlers arrived here. According to Gomez, "They showed up two years later in 1834, with the land lottery deed and with Georgia soldiers saying, 'I've got this land from the lottery. Get off of it.'"

Another small constitutional violation that was part of the land grab: Georgia seized the Cherokee printing press, so they couldn't publicize their cause and win political support in states up north.

No one annoyed Jackson like Principal Chief John Ross. Ross was a Jeffersonian figure in almost every sense. A founding father of the Cherokee Nation in its modern, legal form, it was Ross who cribbed from Jefferson in writing the Cherokee constitution. Like Jefferson, he preached liberty while owning slaves. An educated gentleman planter, Ross was only one-eighth Cherokee—just one-eighth, even I'm more Cherokee than that—but he was their chief from 1827 to 1866. Toward the end of his life he corresponded with Abraham Lincoln; in his early years, he was such a believer in the inherent justice of the American system that he lobbied relentlessly in Washington, D.C.,

believing that once Congress and the president understood that the
Constitution applied to this virtuous, sibling republic, they would
treat the tribe fairly, as equals.

Once the state of Georgia began evicting the Cherokee, and John
Ross among them, Ross wrote, "Treated like dogs, we find ourselves
fugitives, vagrants, and strangers in our own country."

The tribe was divided about what to do: stay and fight or demand
cash for the land and head west. No one exploited this split more than
Andrew Jackson.

The majority of the tribe wanted to stay put and supported Ross. But
around a hundred men—including *Phoenix* editor Elias Boudinot and
his brother Stand Watie; a hundred in a tribe of sixteen thousand—met
at Boudinot's house in New Echota in 1835 and signed a treaty with the
U.S. government. They had no authority to do this. Called the Treaty of
New Echota, it relinquished all Cherokee lands east of the Mississippi
in exchange for land in the West. They figured, Georgia was already
seizing Cherokee land; this might be the only way the Cherokee would
get something for it.

John Ross, whom the Georgia militia arrested so that he could not
protest, was stunned. He accused the treaty party of treason. The rest
of the sixteen thousand Cherokee signed a petition calling the treaty
invalid and illegal. Congress ratified the treaty by only one vote, despite impassioned pleas on behalf of the Cherokee by Congressmen
Henry Clay and Davy Crockett. The tribe was given three years to remove themselves to the West.

We're now standing at the site of Elias Boudinot's house, where the infamous New Echota treaty was signed. Gomez says, "The spring of '38 rolled around, and nobody was going anywhere. The state of Georgia and the federal government thought they were going to have some problems and you had about seven thousand troops come in to forcibly remove the Cherokees from their farms, from their houses, and initially rounded them up in stockades and moved them up into eastern Tennessee and northeastern Alabama to three immigration depots where they were moved out onto the Trail of Tears as everybody knows it. Technically this is the starting point for the Trail of Tears. For the individual Cherokees, it really started at their front door wherever they were rounded up from."

Amy and I want to step on it, this patch of grass where the treaty was signed, but we hesitate. "It's not a grave," Gomez tells us. But that's what it feels like. We tiptoe onto it, this profane ground. And then we tiptoe away.

As Amy and I travel the Trail of Tears I wonder if we should be embarrassed by certain discrepancies between our trail and theirs. We're weak, we're decadent, we're Americans. Which means: road trip history buffs one minute, amnesiacs the next. We want to remember. Except when we want to forget.

We register at the Chattanooga Choo Choo. Yes, yes, *the* Chattanooga Choo Choo, track 29! It's a hotel now, a gloriously hokey, beautifully restored Holiday Inn, in which the lobby is the ornate dome of the old train station, and the rooms are turn-of-the-century rail cars parked out on the tracks. We're in giggles the entire night for the simple reason that the phrase "choo choo" is completely addictive. We try to work it into every sentence: "What should we do for dinner? Stay here at the Choo Choo?" We end up going out for barbecue, saying, "This is good, but I can't wait to get back to the Choo Choo." We watch *The X-Files* in our train car, commenting, "Is it just me, or is this show even better in the Choo Choo?" I send email from my laptop just so I can write, "Greetings from the Chattanooga Choo Choo Exclamation Point."

Sadly, we check out of the Choo Choo and drive across town to Ross's Landing. It used to be where John Ross's ferry service carried people across the Tennessee River. But in 1838, it was one of the starting points for the water route of the Trail of Tears.

And anchored there, at the river, like some ghost ship, in the very spot where Cherokees were herded into flatboats by the U.S. military, is a U.S. Coast Guard boat. I stand on the sand and read a weathered historical marker: "Established about 1816 by John Ross some 370 yards east of this point, it consisted of a ferry, warehouse and landing. Cherokee parties left for the West in 1838, the same year the growing community took the name Chattanooga."

I'm sure there's no connection at all between those two points. That sounds so nice. They "left for the West." Bye-bye! Bon voyage!

Ross's Landing also functions as Chattanooga's tourist center. Up the hill from the river is the gigantic Tennessee Aquarium and an IMAX theater. The place is crawling with tourists—a crowd so generic and indistinguishable from one another they swirled around us as a single T-shirt.

One hundred and sixty years ago, thousands of Cherokees came through this site. In the summer of 1838, they were forced onto boats and faced heat exhaustion, and then later a drought that stranded them without water to drink. In the fall, they headed west by foot, eventually trudging barefoot through blizzards. Either way, they perished of starvation, dysentery, diarrhea, and fatigue. A quarter of the tribe was dead.

Here, in the shadow of the aquarium, the Trail of Tears is remembered by a series of quotations from disgruntled Native Americans, carved into a concrete plaza. One of the citations, from a Cherokee named Dragging Canoe, is from 1776: "The white men have almost surrounded us, leaving us only a little plot of land to stand upon. And it seems to be their intention to destroy us as a nation."

Good call.

We're moving diagonally across the sidewalk, and happily step on the words of Andrew Jackson, from 1820: "It is high time to do away with the farce of treating with Indian tribes as separate nations."

Amy looks up from the brochure she's reading and says, "These cracks in the sidewalks, they are symbolic of broken promises."

"Are you making that up?"

"No. It says right here, 'Some of the pavement is cracked to symbolize the broken promises made to the Indians.' "

Most Americans have had this experience, most of us can name things our country has done that we find shameful, from the travesties everybody agrees were wrong—the Japanese internment camps or the late date of slavery's abolition—to murkier, partisan arguments about legalized abortion or the *Enola Gay*. World history has been a bloody business from the get-go, but the nausea we're suffering standing on the broken promises at Ross's Landing is peculiar to a democracy. Because in a democracy, we're all responsible for our government's actions, because we're responsible for electing the government. Even if we, the people, don't do anything wrong, we put the wrongdoers in power.

Another piece of the sidewalk quotes a letter from Ralph Waldo Emerson to President Martin Van Buren (who, playing George Bush to Jackson's Ronald Reagan, enforced his predecessor's removal policy) in 1838. "A crime is projected that confounds our understandings by its magnitude. A crime that really deprives us as well as the Cherokee of a country. For how could we call the conspiracy that should crush these poor Indians our government, or the land that was cursed by their parting and dying imprecations our country any more? You, sir, will bring down the renowned chair in which you sit into infamy if your seal is set to this instrument of perfidy. And the name of this nation, hitherto the sweet omen of religion and liberty, will stink to the world."

The path ends with a quotation from an unknown survivor of the Trail of Tears who said, "Long time we travel on way to new land. People feel bad when they leave old nation. Womens cry and make sad wails. Children. And many men. And all look sad like when friends die. They say nothing and just put heads down and keep on go towards west. Many days pass and people die very much. We bury close by trail."

That last passage, especially the part about "when friends die," brings Amy and me to tears. And we just stand there, looking off toward the Tennessee, brokenhearted. Meanwhile, there are little kids literally walking over these words, playing on them, making noise, having fun. We sort of hate them for a second. I ask a teacher who's with a group of fourth graders why she isn't talking to them about Cherokee history. She says normally she would, but it's the end of the school year, this trip is their reward for being good. It seems reasonable.

I ask Amy if she thinks these kids should share our sadness. She says, "I think it's a sad story. It's sort of like the Holocaust. You don't have to be Jewish to think that's definitely a sad part of history. And I think the Trail of Tears is America's version of genocide. Really, it started right over there."

Still, I can't take my eyes off those children. I envy them. I want to join them. I wanted to come on this trip to get a feel for this trail that made us; standing at Ross's Landing, it hits me how crazy that is—how crazy I was. Suddenly the only thing I get out of it is rage.

Why should we keep going?

I don't know. I seriously don't. I know it's an interesting story and I'm supposed to be interested in my past, but what good comes of that?

I'm feeling haunted, weighed down, in pain. This might have been a mistake. It isn't a story where the more you know, the better you'll feel. It's the opposite. The more I learn, the worse I feel. This trip is forcing me to stand here next to a stupid aquarium and hate the country that I still love.

There are only so many hours a human being can stomach unfocused dread. I was tired and confused and depressed and I needed the kind of respite that can only come from focused resentment. In the Trail of Tears saga, if there's one person you're allowed to hate, it's Andrew Jackson, the architect of the Indian removal policy. And since the trail passed through Nashville anyway, we stop at his plantation, the Hermitage. We get a private tour from Hermitage employee Carolyn Brackett. The house and museum are closed to the public when we arrive because of astonishing tornado damage. All the trees are down. Part of me wanted to destroy Andrew Jackson and everything representing him. Seeing all those hacked-up trees made me feel like Someone had beaten me to the punch.

Inside, there's no display mentioning Indian removal because, remarkably, there is no display about Jackson's presidency. Carolyn Brackett showed us around the house, a columned antebellum mansion that looks like a cross between Graceland and Tara. Unfortunately for my spite spree, I liked Carolyn Brackett a lot and I felt bad for her. She would point into the library and say Jackson subscribed to a lot of newspapers before his death, and I'd say, "Was one of them the *Cherokee Phoenix*?" Brackett wasn't sure.

Brackett points into a room and says, "All of the rooms that have original wallpaper, all of the paper was conserved and had to be cleaned with an eraser the size of a pencil eraser. So that was quite an undertaking." She points to a painting of Jackson that "was finished nine days before his death. I think he shows the wear and tear of his life in that portrait."

He looks like he's sticking his head out a car window.

Brackett agrees, "I guess he wasn't worrying about his hair much by then."

Brackett guides us past the flower garden planted by Jackson's wife, Rachel, and into the family graveyard. There are a few piddly head-stones and one Greco-Roman monstrosity with an obelisk rising from the center.

"He actually had this designed for Rachel and left room for other family members," Brackett says as she leads us onto Jackson's grave.

I pull a book out of my backpack, a book with the subtitle *Andrew Jackson and the Subjugation of the American Indian*. Carolyn Brackett and Amy exchange a worried look.

I tell her that I'm standing here on Andrew Jackson's grave and that as a person of partly Cherokee descent, I wouldn't mind dancing on it. I read her a letter that Jackson wrote about the removal of the south-eastern tribes. It says, "Doubtless it will be painful to leave the graves of their fathers, but what do they more than our ancestors did nor than our children are doing? To better their condition in an unknown land our forefathers left all that was dear in earthly objects. Our children by thousands yearly leave the lands of their birth to seek new homes in distant regions." And then it ends, "Can it be cruel in the Government, when, by events which it cannot control, the Indian is made discontent in his ancient home to purchase his lands, to give a new and extensive territory, to pay the expense of his removal, and support him a year in his new abode. How many thousands of our own people would gladly embrace the opportunity of removing to the West on such conditions?"

There's something nutty about Old Hickory in this passage. Just the fact that he compares the *removal* of Indians from their land with the *opportunity* of his generation to just go out west. I ask Brackett if she can help me understand his mindset.

"Probably not," she sighs. "The interesting thing about that era was that they really felt that they were preserving. This is how they justified it in their own minds. That this was inevitable. It was sort of the early thought of manifest destiny. They never really seemed to think that we were going to settle the country all the way to the West, all the way to California. So if they just kept moving everybody further away, they'd eventually get to a point where there wasn't going to be any settlement, which, of course, didn't happen."

A few minutes after we pull out of the Hermitage's driveway, we're on the highway that cuts through Nashville. I regard even the most garish of the Opryland billboards with what can only be called warmth. Like a lot of people born in the South and the southern backwater states of Texas, Arkansas, and Oklahoma, Amy and I watched the *Grand*

Ole Opry on television as children. While other kids our age spent the 1970s banging their heads to Kiss doing "Rock and Roll All Nite," we were humming along with "The Tennessee Waltz." Nashville, not Washington, was our cultural capital, home to heroes like George Jones, Ernest Tubb, and Loretta Lynn.

Carolyn Brackett had told us that most of the visitors to the Jackson plantation were spillover tourists from Nashville's country music attractions. Watching the billboards go by, I'm beginning to realize that maybe that is not such a coincidence. My heart sinks. I want to hate Andrew Jackson because it's convenient. I need one comforting little fact, one bad guy in a black hat to aim my grief at. But there's another Andrew Jackson nagging at me, the adjective, the one who lent his name to Jacksonian democracy, a fine idea.

Jackson was the first riffraff president. Washington, Jefferson, Madison, Monroe, and the two Adamses all came from patrician colonial families. They were gentlemen. Jackson, on the other hand, was a bloodthirsty, obnoxious frontiersman of Irish descent, a little bit country, a little bit rock 'n' roll. And no matter what horrific Jackson administration policy I point out, I can't escape the symbolism of Jackson's election. The American dream that anyone can become president begins with him.

My sister and I disapprove of what Jackson did to our people, but the fact is, Jackson is our people too. We also come from that *Opry*-watching segment of the population which the nicer academics euphemistically refer to as "working class" and the nastier television comics call "white trash." This is a race which a friend once described to me as "being Scotch or Irish plus at least three other things." Which is us. It wasn't anything anyone in our family ever talked about, it was just something I sensed. I first confronted it when I was eleven and read *Gone with the Wind*. I had the exact same reaction to the book as the young protagonist in Dorothy Allison's novel *Bastard Out of Carolina*: "Emma Slattery, I thought. That's who I'd be, that's who we were. Not Scarlett with her baking-powder cheeks. I was part of the trash down in the mud-stained cabins . . . stupid, coarse, born to shame and death."

Andrew Jackson was partly about being born to shame and death and becoming president anyway. That part of his biography is thrilling just as the similar glory chapters in the biographies of Elvis and Bill Clinton are thrilling. I don't know how it felt to be a poor redneck out in the middle of nowhere when Jackson got elected, but I do know what it felt like the day a man certain Easterners dismissed as a cracker beat that silver spoon George Bush. Personally, I felt like they just handed my Okie uncle Hoy the keys to Air Force One.

That Jackson's election was a triumph of populism still does not negate his responsibility for the Trail of Tears. If anything, it makes the story that much darker. Isn't it more horrible when a so-called man of the people sends so many people to their deaths? One expects that of despots, not democrats.

We drive on into Kentucky, toward Hopkinsville. When the Trail of Tears passed through southern Kentucky in December of 1838, a traveler from Maine happened upon a group of Cherokees. He wrote, "We found them in the forest camped for the night by the road side . . . under a severe fall of rain accompanied by heavy wind. With their canvas for a shield from the inclemency of the weather, and the cold wet ground for a resting place, after the fatigue of the day, they spent the night. Several were then quite ill, and an aged man we were informed was then in the last struggles of death. . . . Even aged females, apparently nearly ready to drop into the grave, were traveling with heavy burdens attached to the back—on the sometimes frozen ground, and the sometimes muddy streets, with no covering for the feet except what nature had given them. We learned from the inhabitants on the road where the Indians passed, that they buried fourteen or fifteen at every stopping place."

John Ross's wife died in a place like this—in winter—of pneumonia. She had one blanket to protect herself from the weather, and she gave it to a sick child during a sleet storm.

It gets worse. I always knew the Cherokee owned slaves, that they owned them in the East and that they owned them in the West. Only in the course of this road trip did it occur to me that the slaves got to Indian territory in the same manner as their masters—on the Trail of Tears. Can you imagine? As if being a slave wasn't bad enough? To be a slave to a tortured Indian made to walk halfway across the continent?

We stopped in Hopkinsville because it was on the map, but pulling into town we saw signs for a Trail of Tears Memorial Park we didn't know about. It seemed like a good idea to go there.

A Shelley Winters ringer named Joyce is sitting on the porch of the little museum, drinking soda. She's one of the volunteers who run the place. When I ask her about the park's origins, she tells us, "Hopkinsville was a ration stop along the way on the Trail of Tears. The Cherokee camped here. They were here for a week or so. While they were here, two of their chiefs died and they're buried up on the hillside. You should start here and walk up to the grave area. There are three bronze plaques on each one of the posts. The first two will give you the story of the Trail of Tears. The last one, just before you go into the grave area, tells you about the two chiefs, Whitepath and Flysmith."

The plaque nearest the graves says that Whitepath was one of the Cherokee who fought under Andrew Jackson in 1814 at the Battle of Horseshoe Bend. Jackson even gave Whitepath a watch for his bravery. In that battle, a Cherokee saved Jackson's life. Which underscores the level of Jackson's betrayal of the tribe. Had a Cherokee not saved his life then, Whitepath and Flysmith might not be buried here beneath our feet.

The graves are on a little hill. You can hear the highway down below, but still it's serene. Up until this moment, all the graves along the trail had been metaphorical. All through Tennessee, Amy and I kept saying, "We're driving over graves, we're driving over graves." But even then, we just imagined them there, under the blacktop, off in the woods. But here, the skeletons suddenly had faces, specific stories. The graves were real.

After Hopkinsville, we drive past farms that look so cliché they're practically pictographs—barns straight out of clip art, the cowiest possible cows. For whole minutes at a time, I convince myself that we're on a normal road trip. But we're not. We're on a death trip, and I can't go more than a few miles without agonizing and picking apart every symbolic nuance of every fact at my disposal. Which Amy might have found charming in Georgia since she hadn't seen me or my obsessions in months, but halfway through Tennessee—right about the second I see her wince in the company of Carolyn Brackett—I can practically hear her silent prayers that I shut up.

I don't know how old we were when we switched roles. As children, she was the loud one, the one with the mood swings, and I was the dutiful, silent observer. At every Trail of Tears site we visit, Amy wants to be the hospitable guest. She says please and thank you, wants to look around in peace. I can see her squirm every time I ask a question. After I cornered Joyce at the Hopkinsville site, she scolded me, "Sarah, it looked like she was on her break."

Back in the car, I try and keep quiet. Joyce had mentioned she gives a lot of tours to school groups. Which sounds like a lot of responsibility. She didn't make a big deal out of it, saying that the students "ask intelligent questions." I wondered if they have a hard time emotionally reconciling the facts of the Trail of Tears. She said, "No, I don't think there's any emotional stress for them at all."

Amy swerves a little when, after half an hour of cow-gazing hush, I burst out, "I think working there would be like working at the Holocaust Museum or working on some restored plantation, work that involves displaying and reliving some kind of senseless evil. I can't imagine having to go there every day. The thing I like about this trip is that it's going to be over fast."

"I don't know, Sarah." It's always a bad sign when Amy says my name. "I don't know how Joyce deals with it. I'm sure she doesn't obsess about it, because otherwise, she would just go crazy." Amy glances away from the road a second to give me the eye, complaining, "I think you catch people off guard. She was just sitting there drinking her Coke and eating her crackers and then you showed up."

"We showed up, Amy," I remind her. "Do you think asking these people questions and prying into what they do, do you think that's wrong?"

"I don't think it's wrong at all to ask people what they think. I just wonder how it would be different if you sent them a letter and said, 'Hey, Joyce, how is it working here?' If she had time to think about it and think about what goes through her mind every day instead of just saying, 'Hey, do you work here? Can you answer some questions?' Because she obviously really, really cared. I mean she was proud of that little place and she should be. And how does she know if the kids have to emotionally grapple with the thing. She just trots them around, shows them this, shows them that, and then they get on the bus and go home."

I bring up another qualm. I get a new one every ten minutes, and this one has nothing to do with blaming America or blaming Andrew

Jackson or blaming the Cherokees who signed the Treaty of New Echota. I'm starting to blame myself, because I have this tiny, petty thought—an embarrassingly selfish gratitude for the Trail of Tears, because without it, my sister and I wouldn't exist.

Amy rolls her eyes. "I don't think four thousand people needed to die so that we could be sitting here today. But it's a fact of not just life, but of our life, so I think we need to come to grips with that—*Sarah.*"

It took the Cherokee about six months to walk to Oklahoma. We're doing it in five days. Every ten minutes, we cover the same amount of ground they covered in a day.

We drive with the sun in our eyes. On back roads, through Kentucky. We duck into a remote, depressed section of downstate Illinois. A plaque marks a spot where thousands of Cherokee camped, unable to cross the Mississippi because of floating ice. We cross in under a minute. I know we're going fast but it doesn't feel fast. We plod through most of Missouri, stopping at yet another Trail of Tears State Park. There's actually a name for what we're doing: Heritage Tourism. Which sounds so grand—like it's going to be one freaking epiphany after another. But after a while we just read the signs without even getting out of the car. At the end of every day, we fall into our motel beds, wrecked.

In the morning, we trudge through Arkansas. We're stuck for two hours behind a Tyson chicken truck, unable to pass. We cruise through the Pea Ridge National Military Park, a Civil War battleground we visited once as children. It was here our great-great-grandfather

Stephen Carlile fought—and lost—under Stand Watie's Confederate regiment of Cherokees. Watie, by the way, was the last Confederate general to surrender; he kept on fighting for two months after Appomattox; fighting was one thing he knew how to do.

We have another one of those twin moments where Amy wonders what it was like for Stand Watie to come back and fight in a spot he passed through on the Trail of Tears and I'm making myself sick trying to reconcile the fact that oppressed Indians could live with owning slaves, to die for slavery's cause.

We're not the only ones touring the park. We're just another car on the road. A lot of Americans do stuff like this every summer—traipse their kids around historic landmarks as a matter of course. Our dad brought us here, hoping to instill a sense of history in us. And even though there's really not that much to see except for a couple of cannons and a field of grass, it worked. We're back, aren't we? Amy and I came to see this history—and this country—as ours. Though as a kid I would've been too carsick and sleepy to imagine that I would someday willingly come back to Pea Ridge of my own accord.

It's just a short hop to Fayetteville. We have lunch with two old roommates of mine, Brad and Leilani, who take us to a little Trail of Tears marker next to a high school parking lot. It says that a thousand Cherokees camped on this spot in the summer of 1839.

The sign's facing a semicircular arrangement of boulders. Anyone who's ever been to high school would recognize it instantly as the place students go to sneak cigarettes or get stoned. And once again it's striking how the two American tendencies exist side by side—to remember our past, and to completely ignore it and have fun. Look at how we treat all our national holidays. Don't we mourn the dead on Memorial Day with volleyball and sunscreen? Don't We the People commemorate the Fourth of July by setting meat and bottle rockets on fire? Which makes a lot of sense when you remember that a phrase as weird and whimsical as "the pursuit of happiness" sits right there—in the second sentence of the founding document of the country.

The most happiness I find on the trip is when we're in the car and I can blare the Chuck Berry tape I brought. We drive the trail where thousands died and I listen to Berry's nimble guitar, to the poetry of place names as he sings "Detroit Chicago Chattanooga Baton Rouge," and I wonder what we're supposed to do with the grisly past. I feel a very righteous anger and bitterness about every historical fact of what the American nation did to the Cherokee.

But at the same time I am an entirely American creature. I'm in love with this song and the country that gave birth to it. Listening to "Back in the U.S.A." while driving the Trail of Tears, I turn it over and over in my head—it's a good country, it's a bad country, good country, bad country. And of course it's both.

When I think about my relationship with America, I feel like a battered wife: Yeah, he knocks me around a lot, but boy, he sure can dance.

Fayetteville's not far from the Oklahoma state line. A sign greets us that reads, "Welcome to Oklahoma, Native America."

Amy says, "I don't remember the signs used to say that."

I tell her that, no, I think they used to say, "Oklahoma is O.K." Which is about right: It's *okay*.

We're now in the western Cherokee Nation. And the maddening thing—the heartbreaking, cruel, sad cold fact—is that northeastern Oklahoma looks *exactly* like northwestern Georgia. Same old trees, same old grassy farmland. The Cherokee walked all this way—crossed rivers, suffered blizzards, buried their dead—and all for what? The same old land they left.

We breeze through Tahlequah, the Cherokee capital. Even though the Trail of Tears officially stops there, our trail won't be over until we get to our hometown—Braggs. It's about twenty minutes away and we plan on spending the evening with our aunts and uncles there. I put in a tape of a teen brother band from Tulsa singing "MMMbop," the first song in the traditional end of Trail of Tears Hanson medley. Of course we don't get to bop for long.

The road out of Tahlequah is called the POW-MIA Highway. The fun doesn't stop! God bless America, and history, too. We finished mapping the Trail of Tears two minutes ago and now we run smack dab into Vietnam, a war, as I recall, that brought the word "quagmire" into popular use. What's next? A billboard screaming, "Honk if you have misgivings about how the FBI handled Waco!"

We turn left onto the two-lane highway that leads to Braggs, my own private quagmire. This is the nineteen miles of road that connects our hometown to the county seat, Muskogee. Amy and I have been on it hundreds if not thousands of times, though only I know its topography with the intimacy that comes from leaning over every inch of it, carsick. I can't help but wonder if the grass grows so close to the shoulder because of my personal fertilizer crusade: I was a little Lady Bird Johnson of puke.

"It's not that far, is it?" Amy asks. "It seemed like it was forever when we were kids to get to Muskogee, didn't it? Because we always got stuff when we got to go there—pizza and movies. What else did we get?"

I got to throw up on the side of the road.

Amy looks up. "Braggs Mountain. Not much of a mountain," she says, a Montanan now.

Not much of a town. We're here. A sign at what could loosely be called the city limits announces, "Welcome to Braggs. Rural Living."

Our aunt Lil and uncle John A.'s house in Braggs smells exactly as I remember it, like cookies. They welcome us with hugs and food. Our aunt Jenny and uncle Hoy, our funniest relatives, are there to see us, too. We sit around the kitchen table in stitches just like always. I've missed this.

After supper, Lil, Jenny, Hoy, and Amy go out and sit on the porch and leave Uncle John A. and me inside to talk. At seventy-four, my mother's brother is my oldest living relative. He's a World War II veteran. I asked him about his great-grandfather Peter Parson, who came to Oklahoma on the Trail of Tears when he was twelve years old.

John A. says that Peter was brought on the trail by two Presbyterian ministers. "He grew up here. And he was a stonemason. Some of his

work is still around Tahlequah. If you're going up to the Village tomorrow," meaning the Cherokee Heritage Center called Tsa-La-Gi, "you'll
see two big columns."

"He built those?"

"He helped build those two columns. See, they built that right after
they came up here."

I didn't know that. The columns he's talking about—and there are
actually three instead of two—are the great symbols of the Cherokee
Nation in the West. For years, I've had an old photograph of the
columns stuck on my refrigerator door. They are all that's left of the
remains of the Cherokee Female Seminary, the very first public school
for girls west of the Mississippi, which my great-grandmother on my
father's side attended.

Everything about the journey until now has been a little world-
historical. Hearing that our ancestor helped build the columns is the
first time I felt an actual familial connection to the story.

I ask John A. about our family and the Cherokee presence in Oklahoma. I ask him a lot of off-topic questions about his service in World
War II, mainly because I was dying to; I was never allowed to ask him
about it when I was a kid, because thirty years after V-J Day, he was still
having nightmares and flashbacks. And then I ask him a mundane, re-
porterly question about whether he thinks the state of Oklahoma has
done a good job educating its students about American Indian history.
He says yes, then jumps into a non sequitur about his own education
that I haven't been able to stop thinking about since.

"I just wish that I could have maybe went to school a lot more. I didn't get no education. That was one of my big faults. But when I was growing up, it took everybody to make a living. I had to work." He says he only got a third-grade education. "Did you know that?"

"No. Third grade."

"That's all I've got," he says. "Third grade. We didn't get no education. So what you learn, you can't afford to forget."

On this trip I've been so wrapped up in all the stories of all the deaths on the Trail of Tears. Sitting there, listening to my uncle ask "what if," I realize that there are lots of ways that lives are pummeled by history.

If the Trail of Tears is a glacier that inched its way west, my uncle is one of the boulders it deposited when it stopped. He had to work the farm, and the farm he worked was what was left of his grandfather's Indian allotment. And then came the Dust Bowl, and then came the war. All these historical forces bore down on him, but he did not break. Still, compared to him, compared to the people we descend from, I am free of history. I'm so free of history I have to get in a car and drive seven states to find it.

Uncle John A. remarks, "It's good to know where you're from. To know where your beginning is. It really, probably, don't amount to all that much. Only just to one's self. It has nothing to do with what you're going to do tomorrow or a week or two from now. But at least, if you want to look back on this trip, and say, 'Well, I was down in the area there where some of my ancestors originated from.' "

The next morning, the columns are the first thing we see when we get to Tsa-La-Gi. The last time we were here, we were nine years old. Not surprisingly, the columns are more diminutive than we remember. We rush over to the amphitheater entrance. We walk past the place where you'd get your programs, and Amy waves hello to the statue of Sequoyah. She points to the stage where the Phoenix would rise again. I point to the spot where Stand Watie was always throwing a fit.

Unfortunately, due to loss of funding the drama here at Tsa-La-Gi won't be performed this summer. Amy and I sit in the chairs where we first learned about the Trail of Tears and talk about our trip. Our experiences were different. She minored in Native American Studies in college. She not only owns a copy of *Black Elk Speaks*, she could quote from it.

For Amy, the trip was about empathy: "I've been pretty close to tears sometimes just thinking about the pain, what the kids must have been thinking. When we were driving, I just kept imagining the kids saying, 'Where are we going? Where are we going? What is happening?' I've just been thinking about what it really must have been like."

I've been thinking about those kids, too. But the person I identify with most in this history is John Ross, because he was caught between the two nations. He believed in the possibilities of the American Constitution enough to make sure the Cherokee had one, too. He believed in the liberties the Declaration of Independence promises, and the civil rights the Constitution ensures. And when the U.S. betrayed not only the Cherokee but its own creed I would guess that John Ross was not only angry, not only outraged, not only confused, I would guess that John Ross was a little brokenhearted.

Because that's how I feel. I've been experiencing the Trail of Tears not as a Cherokee, but as an American.

John Ridge, one of the signers of the Treaty of New Echota, once prophesied, "Cherokee blood, if not destroyed, will wind its courses in beings of fair complexions, who will read that their ancestors became civilized under the frowns of misfortune, and the causes of their enemies." He was talking about people like my sister and me. The story of the Trail of Tears, like the story of America, is as complicated as our Cherokee-Swedish-Scottish-English-French-Seminole family tree. Just as our blood will never be pure, the Trail of Tears will never make sense.

Ixnay on the My Way

As 1997 wore on, I considered changing the message on my answering machine to "Frank Sinatra deathwatch." Thanks mostly to a little essay I wrote in February of that year called "Ixnay on the My Way"—a plea to television producers not to rehash my least favorite song in their inevitable obituary segments—friends and acquaintances kept calling, leaving bulletins like "He's in the hospital again" or "I heard that he's a goner for real." An editor I had promised a proper, postmortem obituary would keep me posted: "I hope you're not too busy this week . . ." If journalist Gay Talese's most famous essay of the '60s was called "Frank Sinatra Has a Cold," my most famous essay of the '90s should have been titled "Frank Sinatra Is Going to Die." Of course, when I heard the news of Sinatra's death on May 15, 1998, I watched TV all day, checking up on the programs I had pleaded with in the essay, and every last one did exactly as I had predicted. It is no fun being right. (Though, in a weird postmodern twist, a version of this story ended up at the end of ABC's

Nightline *that night, functioning in TVland as something of a last word.) Perhaps "Ixnay on the My Way" became irrelevant the moment it came true. But ultimately, I don't think it's about Frank Sinatra as much as it is about television news: What if they're giving us the cheap and lazy "My Way" obit version of every story they report?*

IS THERE ANYTHING NICER THAN A REALLY GOOD TV OBITUARY? ANY DAY now, Peter Jennings will cut away from some freak mudslide story (casualties: six registered voters), face another camera, and announce Frank Sinatra's death. Later, the *World News Tonight* credits will roll over a tasteful montage of Frank's film stills and album covers. The other networks will run similar tributes, as will the brainiacs at *Entertainment Tonight* and those swingers on *The NewsHour* at PBS. But you know what? It will not matter whether Sinatra's video wake is hosted by the tweedy Jim Lehrer or the perky Katie Couric. Because each and every remembrance will be accompanied by the same damn song: the most obvious, unsubtle, disconcertingly dictatorial chestnut in the old man's vast and dazzling backlog. "My Way."

When the guy who generously gave us greats like "I Get a Kick out of You" kicks it, we won't put on our Basie boots or get a load of those cuckoo things he's been sayin'. We'll be bored terrif-ically, screaming at the TV set every time he and that sappy string section face the final curtain. Get it? He's dead *and* on tape from the grave talking about "how the end is near." Spooky.

The only way "My Way" has ever worked is if the person singing it is dumber than the song. Which is why the only successful rendition of it was perpetrated by Sid Vicious. Frank, and Elvis for that matter, was always too complicated, too full of rhythmic freedom to settle into the song's simplistic selfishness. "My Way" pretends to speak up for self-possession and personal vision when really, it only calls forth the temper tantrums of two-year-olds—or perhaps the last words spoken to Eva Braun.

Toward the end of 1996, there were rumors from Belgrade that each night when the government-controlled evening news was on, the townspeople blew whistles or banged on pots and pans so they wouldn't hear the state's lies. Keep that beautiful action in mind when Sinatra's dead and all the TVs in your more boring democratic world are playing "My Way." Drown it out. Play something else to the montage in your own heart. Or just turn off the TV sound. Have your stereo cued up and ready to go. He could keel over any second. Be prepared!

Why not play "Angel Eyes" for its subtle reference to the singer's Mediterranean windows to the soul, for its knowing jaunty adieu: " 'Scuse me, while I disappear." Are you with me, Peter Jennings? Think about how great that would work under all those postwar, black-and-white snapshots, how that nice Christian harp outro hints at Frank's unlikely salvation.

I admit, "Angel Eyes" may not be quite stupid and obvious enough for network television. So for the staff of the *Today* show, here's another suggestion: "That's Life." If "Angel Eyes" is all periods and pauses, this song is all Exclamation Points!!!!!!! Picture quick-cut shots of Sinatra with Ava Gardner, Sinatra with daughter Nancy, Sinatra with Kennedy, Sinatra with some mob boss no one will recognize anyway, while the singer belts his résumé, "I've been a puppet, a pauper, a pirate, a poet, a pawn, and a king." "That's Life" is a terrible choice, just as corny as "My Way." But at least it's got a little bit of the old ring-a-ding-ding.

As for me, when I hear the big news, I'm tempted to think I'll be cranking up my favorite Sinatra side, "Come Dance with Me." But it's too disrespectfully cheerful to work as a dirge and kind of creepy if taken literally. Who except Tom Petty wants to fox-trot with a corpse?

I've decided instead to blare the Capitol recording of Cole Porter's "What Is This Thing Called Love." It's the driving question behind the entire Sinatra research project. And it's a lovely pop song, suitably melancholy for mourning, reflective, and wise. The orchestra starts off low. Enter a clarinet that's somehow lewd and ponderous at the same time. Frank scrawls the topic sentence, then repeats it, adding one word—this *funny* thing called love. It begins as a rhetorical question and, by the end, turns into a cosmic inquiry of God. At the end of the song, Frank asks "the Lord in heaven above" its question and then he cuts out, as if he's off to face the Creator in person. And then, once he's gone, the orchestra resolves to a sweet final chord, as if they have the answer, but Frank Sinatra's no longer around to hear it.

Can't you just see the freeze-frame? Frank, in the recording studio, the hat askew, the tie loosened? TV producers of America, I beg you—for all of us, for Frank—ixnay on the "My Way."

M I X   T A P E S

Thanks for the Memorex

LONG DISTANCE LOVE AFFAIR BY CASSETTE TAPE: IT HAPPENED TO ME. WHILE digital romances grow increasingly common, our strange fling was quaintly analog. We talked on the phone for hours and enjoyed the occasional mushy rendezvous in the flesh at airports and bookstores and bars. But mostly, we wore out the heads on our respective tape decks compiling Memorex mash notes. I'm not really the scented envelope kind of girl, preferring instead to send yellow Jiffylite mailers packed with whatever song is on my mind.

The most interesting thing about the correspondence was that we rarely agreed. While we cared for each other, we cared little for each other's taste in music. I sent him lovey-dovey lullabies like Blondie's "In the Flesh" and he sent me back what could have been field recordings of amplified ant farms by bands with names like Aphex Twin and Jarboe. I sent him the Jonathan Richman song that goes "If the music's gonna move me it's gotta be action-packed," but he didn't take the hint, sending back music that was almost uniformly action-*lacked*. I think my scrappy little pop songs got on his nerves, and his techno-ambient soundscapes left me impatient for something, *anything*, to happen. Still, I gritted my teeth through them all, groaning over every last spacy synth jam as if I were doing him some kind of personal favor. Since he went to the trouble of making the tape, the least I could do was sit there and take it.

I liked picturing him in his little house, flipping through records and putting them on, taking them off and timing out the cassette so he could fill it up as much as possible but still avoid those immoral endings in which the sound gets cut off in the middle. Just as I liked running around my little apartment trying to remember, say, every rock song that ever had an accordion in it and whether the keyboardless concertina counts.

After a while, the question we asked each other about the tapes we sent wasn't "Did you like it?" The question was "Did you *get* it?" Because receipt ultimately took on more importance than pleasure, and that was perhaps the most telling note. Not that I miss those "songs" of his since we parted ways—not by a long shot. (The letters were good. Those I miss. He quoted James Baldwin a lot. And the phone calls were sweet. I fell in love with him on the phone. He had a soothing voice. A couple of times he called the second he'd finished reading a novel and just had to tell me about it, and I know it sounds hokey and librarian-ish to say so, but I just *swooned* when he did that.)

That music of his did not bother me when we were making out on a bench in front of the La Brea Tar Pits or the alley behind my favorite Chicago bar. It bothered me in those ponderous solitary moments when I asked myself if I could really love a man who did not think, as I do, that a band with two drummers playing two drum sets was some kind of mortal sin, just as I'm sure he asked himself if such a free-wheeling, free-jazz, open mind as himself could really fall for such an oldfangled, verse-chorus-verse relic like me. Which might be shallow, but our incompatible music pointed to incompatible world views. He was the ocean, preferring waves of sound to wash over him with no beginning, middle, or end. I'm more of a garden hose, fancying short bursts of emotion that are aimed somewhere and get turned on and off real quick.

A couple of days after the last time I saw him, I got a typically well-written postcard. He said that after he kissed me goodbye at LAX he was driving away and turned on the radio. Elvis was singing "It's Now or Never." In my personal religion, a faith cobbled together out of pop songs and books and movies, there is nothing closer to a sign from God than Elvis Presley telling you "tomorrow will be too late" at precisely the moment you drop off a girl you're not sure you want to drop off. Sitting on the stairs to my apartment, I read that card and wept. It said he heard the song and thought about running after me. But he didn't. And just as well—those mixed-faith marriages hardly ever work. An Elvis song coming out of the radio wasn't a sign from God to him, it was just another one of those corny pop tunes he could live without.

What I did get out of the entire sad situation, besides big phone bills, a box of cassettes I'll never touch again, and a newfound appreciation for the short stories of Denis Johnson—especially the sentence in *Jesus' Son* that says, "The cards were scattered on the table, face up, face down, and they seemed to foretell that whatever we did to one another would be washed away by liquor or explained away by sad songs," which was pretty prophetic considering that the two men I took up with after my heart was broken were Jack Daniel and Neil Young—was a lingering sentimentality about the act of taping itself. A homemade tape is a work of friendship, an act of love.

I was reminded of that when I was reading Nick Hornby's novel *High Fidelity*. One of the subtexts of his story is the emotional complexities of the taping ritual. Much of the book takes place in a London record store. Clerks Barry and Dick are emotional cripples stuck in that mostly male pop culture circle of hell in which having seen a film (the right kind) or owning a record (ditto) acts as a substitute for being able to express what these things mean to them. Since they are incapable of really talking about human feelings, they get by on standing next to each other at rock shows and making each other complicated tapes of obscure songs.

Rob, their boss at the record store, met his girlfriend Laura when he was a DJ at a dance club. She first approached him because she liked a song he was playing called "Got to Get You Off My Mind." Rob woos Laura by making her a compilation tape, claiming, "I spent hours putting that cassette together. To me, making a tape is like writing a letter—there's a lot of erasing and rethinking and starting again. A good compilation tape, like breaking up, is hard to do. You've got to kick off with a corker, to hold the attention (I started with 'Got to Get You Off My Mind,' but then realized that she might not get any further than track one, side one if I delivered what she wanted straightaway, so I buried it in the middle of side two), and then you've got to up it a notch, or cool it a notch, and you can't have white music and black music together, unless the white music sounds like black music, and you can't have two tracks by the same artist side by side, unless you've done the whole thing in pairs and . . . oh, there are loads of rules."

While I was reading Hornby's book, I happened to glance at an ad in *San Francisco Weekly* that read, "I'll tape record albums for you. Reasonable rates, excellent service. Pick-up available. Bob." And it gave a phone number. Prostitution! That's what I thought, anyway. Paying someone to make a tape for you seems a whole lot like paying someone for a kiss. It is traditional to cover for one's inability to articulate feelings of love through store-bought greeting cards. It's another thing entirely to pass off a purchased compilation tape, a form which is inherently amateur and therefore more heartfelt. To spend money on such a tape would be a crime against love. Aphrodite herself might rise from the ocean to conk such a criminal on the head with the seashell she rode in on.

I asked Hornby what his music-mad record clerks would think if they saw Bob's ad in the paper. "Their public view would be that it's a terrible, awful job for a grown man to do, and why haven't all these people got their own turntables? But I think maybe they'd think secretly it was kind of a neat job and they'd like to sit at home all day taping other people's records."

I called the number in the ad and talked to Bob, a very nice, sane person actually. I expressed my reservations about his work using subtle, professional phrases such as "What a weird job!" Bob explains that by taping his clients' old Dottie West and Frank Sinatra Jr. records, he "brings to life something that was essentially lying dormant in their life. I see it as providing a service that people are happy to pay for. They think it's worth the money. I feel great, make a little money on the side. No problem."

So Bob's business is much more businesslike than I imagined. He doesn't make the kind of painstaking mix tapes you make for someone you have a crush on. "Actually," Bob points out, "people call me and they're so delighted that this service exists that they're super happy and almost not even that price sensitive." His rates vary depending on the quantity of taping his clients demand. He says each tape costs, on average, about ten dollars. Hardly prostitution, more like giving it away.

Still, I remained fascinated by the unsavory if fictional idea that someone might be willing to pay someone else good money to make a compilation tape for his or her loved one. I decided I wanted the job. I had heard that my friend Dave has a new lady in his life, so I roped him into hiring me to make a tape for her.

"It honestly would be a good idea," said my client during our first consultation.

"You're at the tape stage?"

"Well, it could use a spark."

"So tell me about her. Let's try and get at who she is. Is she a femme fatale kind of girl, or more of a my funny valentine?"

He cringed. "Oh God. In sort of a scary way, she's maybe too much of a carbon copy of me."

"And are you a femme fatale, Dave?"

"No. I wouldn't say either one of those. It's not a saccharine, sweet thing. It's kind of low-key."

I wanted to know how intense he feels about this girl, hoping that the term "low-key" wouldn't come up again. I ran some iconic song titles by him so he can decide how far to go with his musical expression of love and/or like. He said that he's okay with "I Wanna Hold Your Hand"; "Let's Spend the Night Together" by the Rolling Stones "has been done"; "Kiss" by Prince is "nice"; though Frank Sinatra singing "Love and Marriage" is nixed because their relationship is "not sentimental. The I-love-you, I-need-you genre would be out. It would be more upbeat, fun stuff than 'Love Me Tender' kind of stuff at this point."

I thought making the tape was going to be easy. If Dave was calling his romance "not sentimental," then he was not having a romance. Thus anything was going to be an improvement. But once I started making Dave's tape, I discovered something I hadn't suspected.

Choosing the songs and their order was sweaty, arduous toil. Making a mix tape isn't like writing a letter, it's like having a job. Without love as the engine of my labor, it was unpleasant. And I discovered something else. I did not want to follow Dave's instructions. Sure, I had worked in the service industry before. I understood its abiding principle, "the customer is always right." At first, I was committed to following Dave's wish not to get too sentimental. I don't know if he's listened to much popular music recorded in the last, oh, half century, but it's pretty gushy stuff. Even though Dave hired me to choose love songs which didn't say I love you, there aren't that many out there. And even if there were, I'm fully confident that his desire for them is dead wrong. My reasoning? He's a boy. I'm a girl. I know better.

Certainly in making the tape I exercised restraint. After all, they've only been together two months. My role in their relationship is important, perhaps pivotal, and I take that responsibility seriously. I want to reassure her, not scare her off. I steered clear of the heavies, avoiding the serious courtship crooner Al Green. I vetoed Elvis, who should, in my opinion, only be employed when you *really* mean it. And when I did invoke Sinatra, I played it safe: not "Taking a Chance on Love" or even "I've Got a Crush on You," but picking instead cheerful, subtle "Let's Get Away from It All" as a low-key, you-and-me-baby, just-the-two-of-us-out-of-town sort of thing. Cole Porter's "Let's Do It" found a place, too. But I went with urbane jokester Noël Coward's live in Las Vegas rendition, in which he moons, "Each man out there shooting craps does it / Davy Crockett in that dreadful cap does it."

Still, despite Dave's request to hold the sugar, the word "love" must pop up something like ninety-eight times over the course of the tape.

So I dropped off the tape at his house and the next day we got together to talk about it.

"I like the tape a lot," he says cheerfully. "There isn't anything that I don't really like."

"I don't know if you noticed or not, but I sort of ditched your instructions. Because you told me not to be too sentimental, and to keep it light and upbeat."

"I thought it was light."

"The word 'love' is bandied about, let's say. Yesterday, you said, the 'I-love-you, I-need-you' genre would be out."

"I did. I don't know where they say that in this tape. Do they?"

"Well, 'I love you' is certainly in there."

"I don't think it is."

But the Raspberries' "Go All the Way" (with the climax, "I need you! I love you! I need you!") is on the tape. Along with Chic's "Give Me the Lovin' " and James Brown's "Hot (I Need to Be Loved Loved Loved)." Can the differences between the way he heard the songs and the way I heard them be attributed to something as cheap and clumsy as a gender cliché? That Dave hears them as songs about sex and I hear them as songs about love? Maybe. But it's not as if I've wanted to marry every man I ever slept with. And since Dave is such a good friend to have, a rememberer of birthdays even, I know firsthand he's not without a certain softness. If we both like the tape, if we both think the tape would make a nice gift for his sweetheart, could the impasse be in the way we're talking about the tape? This being my story, however, I get to like the way I talk about it better. Even if James Brown hollers the verb "love" as a radio-friendly way of saying "fuck" I don't think he means it unsentimentally. James Brown is not, and never was, "low-key."

Anyway, the argument might be moot.

"We got into some sort of fight this morning," he confesses.

"So now you need a tape."

"Yeah. Maybe. I don't know what's up, actually."

I know exactly what's up. Dave has a problem that all the love songs in the world couldn't solve. Dave has a problem that could not be solved even by a one-hundred-minute, Chet Baker/Al Green/Elvis Presley medley recorded on a master-quality, super low-noise, high-bias, five-dollar cassette played in the moonlight as he asks her to dance. His love affair was too far gone before I ever pushed record and play on his behalf. It isn't that Dave is necessarily unsentimental. It's that he's unsentimental about her. He liked the songs I picked. He just didn't mean what the songs said. I can make a tape of "I Believe in Miracles" but I cannot perform miracles.

Drive Through Please

WHEN SOMEONE ASKS ME WHY I DON'T DRIVE, I USUALLY SAY THAT MY sister drives. Which sounds a little loony. But my sister, Amy, and I are twins. The downside of being a twin involves the sharing of attention, affection, and, especially for those born in December, gifts. "Happy Birthday and Merry Christmas, Amy and Sarah!" exclaimed many a box with a single toy inside. The advantage is that twins share responsibilities. There is little or no pressure to become a whole person, which creates a very clear, very liberating division of labor. I did the indoor things, she did the outdoor ones. She learned to ride a bike before I did. I learned to read before she did. She owns at least three pairs of skis. I own at least three brands of bourbon. Driving was her jurisdiction. Criticizing her driving was mine.

"But aren't you from Montana?" the still-unconvinced inquisitor will usually ask. Yes, I'm from Montana, I'll say, a very big state full of very small towns, towns so small that one may walk everywhere.

The next question is always, "Still, aren't you a journalist? Don't journalists need to drive to their stories?" I suppose they do, if they're interviewing bigamists in rural Utah, but not if they live two blocks from an el stop in Chicago and write book reviews in their pajamas. On the four or five days a year when I have to wear shoes to do my job, it has been my experience that the friendly folks at Condé Nast and Public Radio International are very generous about reimbursing cab receipts. If this fails to convince, I bring out my secret weapon, announcing with portentous deliberation that Barbara. Damn. Walters. Does. Not. Drive. Heard of her?

This sort of accusatory conversation, of course, almost never goes down with native New Yorkers, people who, like Barbara Walters, live in that barbaric third world country that is Manhattan, and thus have yet to hear of newfangled American advances like automobiles, happiness, and yards.

In the United States of America, however, if you have reached the age of seventeen without obtaining a driver's license, you get used to The Look. Once a new acquaintance watches you buy beer with a passport, that person will ogle you with the kind of condescending, frightened glance usually reserved for unwed pregnant teenagers. Like you're not a person but instead a kind of sociological statistic, sucking the taxpayers with your moochy demands of food stamps and public transportation. I have seen that look. And, walking home from the grocery store laden with plastic bags, I have heard the voice, too, the

voice screaming from the window of a Honda, graciously advising me
to "get a fucking car."

Nothing scares me more than driving. I can't even ride a bike without mangling my digits and hitting parked cars. I've always been terrified that I'd get behind the wheel and it would turn into one of those
death scenes in a Shangri-Las song with bystanders screaming,
"Lookoutlookoutlookoutlookout!"

In most families, I hear, the father teaches the kids to drive. But I
had been in the backseat when he was screaming at Amy not to damage the U-joints, whatever those are. I figured he already had plenty
of reasons to yell at me without adding car damage to his list of be-
havioral complaints. So Amy tried to teach me—once. Before I even
got around to turning the key in the ignition I couldn't stop giggling
so she kicked me out of her car and made me walk. After that, I
blocked the possibility of driving out of my mind. I'm never going to
drive, like I'm never going to murder anyone, like I'm never going to
like Celine Dion.

What possessed me, then, at the age of twenty-eight, to learn how
to drive? Maybe I agreed to learn because the person who was going
to teach me was my boss on the radio show I work for, Ira Glass. While
learning to drive has dramatic, once-in-a-lifetime, overcoming-
adversity consequences, Ira Glass telling me what to do is a quotidian
routine. If my editor is teaching me, I reasoned, I won't really be
learning how to drive, I'll be working on a story. Working on a story

isn't really life, unless your life happens to involve getting paid to talk to your parents or Burt Bacharach. Or maybe rethinking driving was just part of the general mind-changing trend of adulthood, part of the same impulse that caused me to reverse my previously held opinions on cucumbers, lipstick, and Neil Young. Or maybe the continuing-education aspect of the lessons appealed to me. After spending twenty years in school, I missed the random learning curve, how one day you're counting haiku syllables and the next day they have you con-structing solar-powered hot dog roasters out of tinfoil. Being a grown-up requires a twelve-month calendar, and that calendar is mostly filled up with doing things you know how to do.

Besides, I tell myself as I study the Illinois "Rules of the Road" pam-phlet, it's not like I'm learning how to swim. I lied when I said that nothing scares me more than driving. At least I'll get into a car. I'm so afraid of drowning that I tend to drink beer in half-pints.

"Rules of the Road" is an alarming, apocalyptic work of literature filled with foreboding information such as "carbon monoxide is a deadly poison" and "if fire is an immediate danger you must *jump clear of the vehicle*" and "if your vehicle runs off the roadway into water but does not sink right away, try to escape through a window." (And if you can't swim?) I am nonplussed about the erratic portrayal of non-drivers, the warnings that "bicyclists may make *unexpected moves*." The language is also transparently right-wing, full of diagrams in which the good car is white while the "Black Car is Breaking the Law," and then there's the *Sieg Heil* salute of a right-turn hand signal, or "the vehicle on the left should yield to the vehicle on the right." This booklet feels like a Wes Craven remake of Leni Riefenstahl's *Triumph of the Will* and reading it made me panic.

So by the time I'm ready to go to the DMV and take the written test, I have worked myself into such a frenzy that I feel as though I've just consumed twelve gallons of coffee. I am twitching and tapping my fingers nonstop, ready to forget the whole thing. I go talk to Ira, hoping he'll let me off the hook. He does not. Instead, he gives me a comforting pep talk about how I look "pre-throwup."

I start ranting against what I like to call the car class. The car class runs the world! The car class is the ruling class! The car class is the class which the American world is set up for! The car class pollutes our world! The car class burns fossil fuels! Normally, I care about fossil fuels as much as everyone else in America, which is to say not at all. But I am so terrified of taking the driving test that I'm looking for any way out. As I leave for the test I feel like I'm off to join a cult.

In Chicago, the Department of Motor Vehicles is the Jonestown, the Heaven's Gate, of the American mainstream. And, just as I never really got lawyer jokes until an attorney made me cry, I finally understand all previous DMV humor—those lines *are* long. Other than the fact that the song on the radio when I come in is "Killing Me Softly," it's pretty uneventful. I pass the test, pay twenty bucks, receive a learner's permit.

The next morning Ira picks me up for my first lesson. He is parked in front of a fire hydrant, a bad sign. We go to an elementary school parking lot and I get behind the wheel. I should point out that it is Saturday morning, so I'm not about to bump into or over any six-year-olds.

I am In the Driver's Seat. How I loathe that little colloquialism. I reach to the right for my seat belt, perpetual passenger that I am, and grab hold of the air. I don't know if my feet should be touching the pedals, how much my legs should be bent. I ask Ira what I'm supposed to see out of the mirror, as if reflected glass were some kind of crazy, newfangled technology. I don't know which way to turn the key in the ignition. Ira patiently answers my questions, pointing out which pedal is the brake, which one's the accelerator. He tells me to give it a little gas. My foot nudges the pedal with the delicacy of a Don Rickles punchline. "We just lurched forward like in *Star Trek*," Ira points out.

I drive in circles. Round and round, over and over. Ira notices that every time I make a turn I stick out my tongue, "like a little kid concentrating really hard on drawing a pony." I make more circles. I turn left a little. I lurch left a lot. It is hypnotic. I am coddled. I am encouraged. My instructor coos, "I'm so impressed. Sarah, you're doing so well." Then, "Don't hit the handicapped people!"

It reminds me of learning to play the piano: In the beginning you look at your hands as much as you look at the sheet music. The difficulty isn't decoding the notes, it's doing it in time, without stopping to think about every little move.

After half an hour in which I play the driving equivalent of "Chopsticks," Ira takes over the wheel again to take us to the next parking lot. I look out the window as he drives. Never in my life have I viewed the nation's roadways through the eyes of a driver. Suddenly, our lane appears so narrow and fraught with danger. My beautiful city of orderly boulevards and responsible fellow citizens has turned into some film noir back alley where you can't trust a soul, where even the parked cars look like they're packing heat and they don't care who knows. Ira, formerly hatless, is now tipping his fedora at a skirt in a doorway, though around here a dame's pretty smile gets you nothing but the jaws of life.

Ira drives past Rosehill Cemetery, exclaiming, "Perfect! No one around. No one you can hurt anyway."

I drive past mausoleums and headstones, past graves dating back to the Civil War. Lucky bastards, to live in an America before cars. It occurs to me that some of the occupants must have died in car accidents.

I sigh. I'm bored. I'm no longer nervous, but I'm not really concentrating. I don't feel like myself. I feel stoned, like someone other than me is skidding in the snow. And then, out of nowhere, another car.

Ira screams, "Signal!"

"I can't."

"Signal!"

I'd forgotten there would be other cars involved. I have problems of my own without worrying about the other drivers. Not just their actions—their actual existence. Now that I'm nervous again, I start giggling. When I'm scared, I laugh. A lot. Another truck passed us in the cemetery and I drive straight off the road. Ira, helpful teacher, points out that I drove straight off the road. He calls me a coward. I tell him that, on the contrary, I was protecting the other car, that driving off the road was a *heroic* move.

I'm such a brand-new driver that I have no habits. Five minutes after I lurched away from the truck, a Buick passes and I am magnetically compelled toward it. Ira grabs the wheel and swerves us away, screaming, "Slow! Slow!"

After an hour in the cemetery, he decides I'm ready to drive among the living. To celebrate, he pops in a tape.

"123456!" yells Jonathan Richman. "Road runner, road runner, going faster miles an hour." He remembered. It's one of my favorite songs. We bicker a minute about what it's about—he says it's about driving, I say it's about listening to the radio—as I slowly navigate a residential street and pull up to big, noisy Western Avenue. The song is so blissfully distracting that I find myself keeping pace with the music and not the traffic. And four cars, in a kind of convergence of hate, honk a big welcome to the car class.

Ira assures me that it was a good first day, though I'm so shook up I drive us straight to a bar where I down three whiskeys. He drives me home.

The next morning Ira shows up for my second lesson. He is ready to go. His readiness is not shared. I refuse to get back into the car. I might never get into a car again. I tell him I can't drive, that I feel removed from the whole thing, that I wasn't driving, I was doing a story.

"You drove for two hours," Ira counters. "But somehow you still think you haven't driven?"

"Well, driving just isn't something I do. I guess I can see that physically, yes, I was doing it and I remember being there and all. But I just felt like that was my evil twin or something."

Ira, trying not to lose his temper, reminds me, "Yesterday, when you and I were in the car, everything was just fine."

"It's only right now you're getting on my nerves."

"That's what I was going to say! Sarah, you're getting on *my* nerves. You are. I just can't believe this. You can actually drive, and maybe this is just very boy, but I showed you how to drive. Now you're turning around and you're telling me that it never happened."

Being irrational can get so inexplicable. I put my foot down: "I don't want to drive. And since I have driven—it feels like I would imagine it feels to have an affair. I feel like I've cheated on myself. You know while you're doing it that that's what you're doing and you can feel yourself touch this foreign object. And the next morning you just wish the whole thing had never happened. You just hope no one ever finds out."

I'm deflated. I need encouragement. Ira launches into an America the Beautiful litany about hitting the road and Dean Moriarty and how "driving *is* America and how there's a fundamental idea of what it is to be an American that's bound up in every on-the-road song and movie and story that I have ever loved, like it's waitin' out there like a killer in the sun, just one more chance we can make it if we run."

I know he's desperate when he starts singing Springsteen, but it doesn't work. I give him this incoherent spiel about driving through "the Monument Valley of the heart" on the "highway within." Not to mention the more pedestrian (ha-ha) argument that American freedom includes the freedom *not* to drive. Besides, Dean Moriarty might have been behind the wheel but the Kerouac character in *On the Road* spent most of the book in the backseat being driven cross-country like the writer he was. He was probably too busy taking notes.

So Ira doesn't get me with Jack Kerouac. He gets me with Jack in the Box.

"Drive-thru," he says.

"Drive-thru? *Really?*"

I know that most people think of the drive-thru as a visual and gastronomic blight. But my sister and I are obsessed with them. Our dad wouldn't go through drive-thrus when we were growing up. I think they make him nervous, partly because he's always been a little deaf. He only approves of fast food when it's served on the fancy trays. So we think of drive-thru as an object of desire, full of thrills denied to us so cruelly for so long.

Ira asks, "So what's it going to be? Do you want Burger King or McDonald's?"

I want to go somewhere on the right-hand side of the street.

Three left turns later, I pull into the drive-thru lane of a Burger King. I cannot believe my luck. I drive up to the menu and the voice takes our order. And he doesn't just say, "Drive through, please." He says, "Drive through, please," to *me.* It is a simple transaction in which I hand the guy some money and he hands me some food, but I am giddy. When he says, "Enjoy your food," I feel like he really means it. It is the best crappy sandwich of my life.

Then I drive off into the sunset. Well, technically, it's afternoon, and I head east, but still. I exit onto Lake Shore Drive, the most beautiful street in America. I merge.

Your Dream, My Nightmare

MY ROCK 'N' ROLL FANTASY IS THAT OCCASIONALLY, EVERY NOW AND then, a song I like comes on the radio. It's a simple dream, I know, and every so often, once or twice a year, it actually comes true. I get all I need from pop music song by song. That's how I like it best—two or three minutes of speed or sorrow coming out of speakers with so much something that the world stops cold.

I've rarely daydreamed of befriending my rock idols. Maybe that's because I tend to admire cranks. Like I really want to toast in the new year with Jerry Lee Lewis or go shoe shopping with Courtney Love or build sand castles with a peach like Lou Reed. My musical heroes are mostly snotty weirdos who didn't become famous because of their social graces. Just because I have them in my heart doesn't mean I want them in my life.

So the very idea of spending five whole days cooped up attending guitar workshops taught by moldy rock big shots (and paying upward of three thousand bucks to do so) at something called Rock 'n' Roll Fantasy Camp is not my fantasy. Try my worst nightmare. I feel compelled to sign up for precisely this reason. What could be more perverse than a headphones-wearing privacy partisan hanging around a bunch of chatty, starstruck record collectors who for all I know might even dance. As I packed a suitcase full of festive black clothes, I remembered the words of my gun-nut father. When I called him a few years ago to make sure he had no ties to the renegade militia called the Freemen, he replied, "Of course not. I'm not a joiner."

Held at the Rat Packish Eden Roc Resort and Spa in Miami, Rock 'n' Roll Fantasy Camp attracted thirty-three participants from all over the United States. Which pop heroes played camp counselor? People whose names you've never known if the years 1970–75 are underrepresented in your record collection in both the chronological and spiritual senses. People like Mark Rivera and Lou Gramm, respectively the saxophonist and lead singer of Foreigner; Mark Farner, the scary, muscled, born-again lead guitarist of Grand Funk Railroad; and Rick Derringer of "Rock and Roll, Hoochie Koo" fame. These names would only attract obsessive liner-note readers, the kind of fans who would thrill at seeking wisdom, not from Billy Joel, but Billy Joel's drummer Liberty DeVitto; not from Bruce Springsteen, but guitarist Nils Lofgren of the E Street Band; not from Peter Frampton, but Bobby Mayo, who played keyboards on *Frampton Comes Alive!*

Campers like Joe, who markets sound equipment in Detroit. Connie and Maxine, sisters from Minneapolis who have left their husbands and kids back home. And Rob, the math teacher from Long Island who heard about the camp on Howard Stern's radio show. Rob gushes, "I love famous people. I like famous people. I love to see and meet famous people, and this is *hanging out* with famous people."

Except for one week at Bible camp in the Ozarks when I was nine—which doesn't really count since my mom was my counselor and my twin sister was my bunkmate and we spent pretty much the whole time praying anyway—I never went to summer camp. Though like all twins I have seen the Hayley Mills movie *The Parent Trap*, in which summer camp is integral to the long-lost-twins plot, at least twenty-five times. So I have a vague notion at the first night's welcoming cocktail party that this is the decisive moment people break off into cliques. Just as Connie and Maxine will end up spending most of their down time with Rob, I find myself befriending two reporters, both named Peter, covering the camp for *People* and *Forbes*. Peter from *Forbes* tells me that when he was a teenager, he walked into a barbershop wearing his Rolling Stones *Some Girls* T-shirt, pointed at Keith Richards's picture, and told the barber he wanted his hair to look like that. I am completely charmed by this, and relieved, because now I have someone I can trust to eat lunch with. Even if he's long since traded in his *Some Girls* clothes for a golf shirt bearing the logo of his wife's law firm.

The first class I attend in the morning is Nils Lofgren's guitar workshop in the Eden Roc basement. It's probably the most low-key, sensible seminar of the camp. Lofgren is a kind, respectful man. Even though he knows what he's doing, he doesn't get all curlicued about it. He pumps out a chugalug rhythm, advising his students to "try to stay in the back pocket of the beat" and "to think like a drummer, real rhythmic." Watching them lurch along is hardly fantastic. It would almost be boring, except that watching nervous people in any given situation is at least slightly engaging. Also, as the only girl in the room, I keep cracking up watching an arrangement of men sitting around in a circle, stroking their instruments. They stroke and stroke and I begin to wonder how long these middle-aged guys can keep this up.

"Usually what I do when my hand starts cramping and I'm getting really frustrated and angry," Lofgren advises, "I stop and play something that's fun. Have you learned the major and minor scales?"

When Lofgren mentions scales, everybody knows the do-re-mi one, but no one knows the blues scale he plays—the most basic downward spiral imaginable. It seems like something you should be paying Kenny down at the Guitar Shack to teach you, instead of bothering the man who pinch-hits for Bruce Springsteen and Neil Young.

Lofgren informs the class that he's going to take a solo and that they should try and "keep the rhythm strong for me." Good luck. What's apparent isn't so much the gaping difference between skill or the lack of it, but rather, the chasm between confidence and self-doubt. Lofgren plays tough, spare riffs and looks so easy-does-it cool. Meanwhile, all the campers around him are tapping their feet like they're marching off to the front lines and all their eyes are fixed on their fingers, trying not to screw up.

As a believer in the anyone-can-do-it, all-or-nothing-at-all ethic of punk rock, I think real music's not about technique or virtuosity. It's about believing in what you have to say and wanting to say it so badly that you'll scream your guts out if that's what it takes to get people to listen. That is my theory. Life, it turns out, is a little more Darwinian.

Later on, when I ask Lofgren if he thought anyone in the camp had real talent—or anything to say—he graciously answers, "I heard a *love* for music in everybody." Love? Is love what Elvis had? Is love what made Kurt Cobain? Observing these random hobbyists try to keep up with Lofgren is like watching *Origin of the Species: The Musical*.

Over the course of the camp, I'll sit through nearly a dozen such seminars. It becomes painfully obvious that rock 'n' roll high school is a lot like real high school. Subject matter doesn't matter as much as the personality of the teacher. Everyone wants to be Lofgren's pet, but Rick Derringer leads his guitar workshop like the nitpick who takes points off for bad penmanship.

"John Alder? Is he here?" Derringer asks, taking attendance. Did he ever imagine, back in his heyday of selling out arenas, that the time would come when he would have to count roll to make sure people showed up to hear him play? After showing off for a while, he proceeds to spend nearly ten whole minutes spreading crackpot ideas. Such as, "I like my guitar to be clean. I find that if you get it all grungy and stuff in between the frets and dirt up here, all of a sudden your arm starts sticking up here. It just doesn't feel the same. I see people sometimes playing, and their guitars are all dirty and the strings are all out of whack. The most important thing is making your guitar playable. So clean the thing. Clean it real good."

"So I do things like"—and here he takes a can out of his guitar case—"Pledge!"

I cannot imagine anyone I admire talking this way. He is holding up a can of furniture polish as if he's doing a TV commercial, reiterating, "Pledge!" Would Keith Richards display a spray bottle of 409? Would Neil Young, asked to discuss his craft, bring up the word "clean"? Isn't the whole point of rock 'n' roll that it's supposed to be the devil's music? That, at heart, it is messy and sweaty and wild? Doesn't Derringer realize that he is uttering such nonsense in a decade whose most influential—and revered and profound—rock movement was called *grunge*, a synonym for filth?

I revere cleanliness—in operating rooms, bathrooms, and restaurants. But public health is one thing, truth and beauty is something else. Derringer probably would have gone up to Martin Luther King Jr. after "I Have a Dream" and said, "Great speech, Dr. King. Too bad it's rendered meaningless by that spinach stuck between your teeth."

While I was gagging at Derringer's dopiness, most of the campers found him hilarious. In fact, these people sat through their workshops and jam sessions and lunch buffets with these serene smiles. Watching them, I got jealous. To me, music has always been an ideological battleground where you hate, hate your enemies and save, save your friends. To them, music seems like this uncomplicated part of their lives that makes them happy or something. As Maxine from Minneapolis puts it, "I'm just here to have some fun and get some exposure to the instruments. I really just like the music."

I am having the quintessential camp experience—homesickness. Most of my days are taken up either wishing I was anywhere but here or pretending to have a good time. Not that I'm incapable of happiness. But I am suspicious of planning for it. My malaise at the camp might not have much to do with musical polemics. Maybe the queasiness I feel watching the campers enjoying themselves has more to do with the fact that I can see they have all kinds of skills I don't have. What if I'm incapable of organized amusement? What if my rock 'n' roll fantasy—the random favorite song on the radio—says less about my taste in music than it does about my taste in life? Doesn't random happiness mean more anyway? What's more exciting, kissing someone after *Casablanca*, a movie which you're more or less legally required to make out after, or fooling around in the middle of the Bobcat Goldthwait vehicle *Shakes the Clown*?

The problem with hanging around the campers was that they were so gosh darn nice. Sweet even. I'm increasingly more embarrassed to realize that I might have come here with malicious intentions, to make fun of the kind of self-satisfied yuppies who could afford such a wacky vacation. But the campers ruined my fun by being so likable. I caught myself muttering Peter Frampton insults under my breath and felt guilty. And you know you're in some kind of parallel universe when the most punk rock person there is the reporter from *Forbes*.

The campers came all this way, paid all this cash. Are they getting their money's worth? One night I cornered Joe from Detroit after dinner. He was just getting out of a limo. "It's the only way to travel," he cracks. He and his family went to dinner with Rick Derringer and Lou Gramm at Gloria Estefan's restaurant. "They were so, so congenial. We had a sing-along in the car. We were doing some Foreigner songs. We were doing 'Hang On, Sloopy.' It was all a cappella and our little kids joined in, too, to help out so it was kind of a group thing—the wives, the kids, the guys."

"Hang On, Sloopy." I'll admit, I love that song. Which came in handy for my sanity. Since Derringer played on it a million years ago with his old band the McCoys, it was constant jam session fodder at the camp. And one night, all the campers gathered onstage to perform it with Derringer singing lead, sparking one of the rare moments when the music they made felt real and sounded exciting—to them and to me.

That kind of excitement didn't last. For every second of participatory, palatable noise, there were three solid hours of rock-star war stories. While I gave myself headaches from rolling my eyes, the campers ate these anecdotes up, egging on people like keyboardist Bobby Mayo to fill their heads with behind-the-scenes insights into *Frampton Comes Alive!*, an album they had apparently memorized note for yucky note.

"We had gotten together as a group in January of that year, '75, and we started touring," Mayo drones. "We were opening for everybody. We opened for ZZ Top, J. Geils, Rod Stewart, Black Sabbath."

If you think listening to this kind of stuff once was boring, try twice. On the camp's last day, goofball Mike Love of the Beach Boys showed up. Every time he opened his mouth it was a defamation of the Beach Boys' greatness. He insulted his audience by telling the same stories at his afternoon lecture as he did onstage the very same night.

In the afternoon, he brags, "I was in India. McCartney's in one bungalow. I'm in the other. We used to have conversations up on the roof at night under the stars. It was pretty cool. He said, 'Mike, you ought to take more care with your album covers.' He was the mastermind behind *Sgt. Pepper's*, right?" In the evening, after a pathetic knockoff of "Barbara Ann," he tells the same story to the same people. "He would say, 'Mike you should take more care with your album covers.' This is the guy who made *Sgt. Pepper's*." Afternoon: " 'With all due respect,' " was his comeback to McCartney, " 'we always paid more attention to what goes *in* the album.' Which is a touché remark, I have to admit." Evening: "So I said, 'Paul. We always took more care with what went *in* them.' It was a touché thing, you'll have to forgive me."

The sad thing is, some people laughed both times. Maybe they were just being nice. They were nice people. Sitting there watching them drink in all those no doubt enhanced rock-star tall tales with such obvious glee was like watching new myths being born. Because anyone with relatives can tell you, rehashed, souped-up stories are not the sole property of washed-up rock stars. I bet Joe from Detroit's going to be telling his Lou Gramm limo story for at least as long as Mike Love's been dissing Paul McCartney. I actually found this reassuring. Once the camp ended, I could go back home to my radio: After a few mornings of sharing the breakfast table with middle-aged sidemen in shorts, the idea of disembodied voices is positively sublime. My nightmare was over the minute I boarded the plane home. But I knew that for the spouses and children and coworkers of the campers, the nightmare had just begun.

Dark Circles

AM HOLDING A BABY PICTURE IN MY HAND—THE PORTRAIT KIND, FROM SEARS. It's me and my twin sister, Amy. We're maybe two, dressed alike. She's crying. Amy's this flashing light—blond hair, blue eyes, white tears. I have one distinguishing characteristic that makes me different from any baby in any picture I've ever seen: dark circles under my eyes. As if I were holding down the swing shift at the tire factory in addition to my official duties as a baby.

My mother says that when I was small she'd wake up in the middle of the night and find me calmly playing with my toys. Once when I was eighteen months old, she got up to check on me and panicked when she saw the front door swinging open. She found me outside crawling around the pasture, giggling. I continued to sneak out as a sleepless teenager. Most nights, I'd go for a walk around three A.M., which was lovely and starlit and safe in Bozeman, Montana. Now I live in Chicago, a city which proudly just edged out New York's murder rate—don't call us the second city—so the three A.M. joy walks aren't an option anymore.

Not that I mind being up at all hours. I give the wee small hours the same extraterrestrial exemptions as airplanes. Just as planes are guilt-free, work-free zones in which to watch Drew Barrymore movies and read *Vanity Fair,* I refuse to do anything productive at four A.M. So until I realize my dream of having an apartment big enough to accommodate a Ping-Pong table, I listen to Elvis or watch TV. Which is amusing when you're visiting old friends such as "Suspicious Minds" or Hitchcock movies for the zillionth time, but less enjoyable the next morning when you wake up after only two good hours of sleep clutching a remote control.

I've had enough. I'm not the advice-seeking, therapy-going, professional-help-getting kind, working under the theory that I know my problems and I'm unwilling to change. But to overthrow insomnia, I pledged to break my personal declarations of independence and ask for help. I'd give it five days, I thought. A work week. I'm can-do when a job's involved.

DAY ONE: MOM

The last time I took advice from my mother I was in high school. She forced me to take a typing class, arguing it might come in handy in later life, and I have never quite forgiven her for being right. But she's a bit of an insomniac herself. I called her up and asked for suggestions on how to handle it.

Mom says, "As I've gotten older, I've learned to drink my herbal tea."

So far so good. Herbal tea: sensible, basic, the boiling of water. Maybe this advice thing isn't as scary as I thought. But Mom's just getting warmed up: "First of all, Sarah, do some serious soul-searching."

Oh, God. I have a policy about that word "soul." It is strictly prohibited except in cases of conversations having to do with okra recipes or Marvin Gaye. My mom doesn't observe these simple, commonsense restrictions. She says, "I want you to get rid of anything that might be bothering you."

"Like my whole life?"

"Your whole life? No, I'm talking about things you need to let go of, things that in the past have upset you or hurt you that you need to let go of. Know what I mean?"

"No. In the New Agey sense? I can't sleep because I have emotional problems?"

She's exasperated. "No, Sarah, I don't think you have emotional problems."

Translation: Yes, Sarah, I do think you have emotional problems.

Normally, any soul-searching on my part is purely accidental—and it's always brought on by a liquid other than herbal tea. I brew some chamomile, telling myself that in the right light it looks a lot like scotch. I sip three cups and search my "soul." More precisely, I search *for* my soul, but I seem to have misplaced it.

So I try something else. I put on a Billie Holiday song and feel like I'm making progress. But when "Why Was I Born?" ends two minutes and forty-eight seconds later, I wonder if I'm confusing introspection with depression.

Soul searching: How do you even know if you're doing it right? How searched is searched?

I take another approach. John Ehrlichman's obituary was just in the paper and I decide to take a personal inventory by comparing my soul with his. Guess what. I come out on top! Do the math with me: The occasional late payment on my college loans . . . Watergate! Forgetting Mother's Day in 1983 . . . Secret bombing of Cambodia! I can't sleep . . . He can't breathe.

I fall into bed immediately and drift off into the sleep of the just. Sadly, I wake up four hours later and never get back to bed. I cross soul-searching and herbal tea off the list. Sorry, Mom.

DAY TWO: THE FRIEND

I ask my friend Barrett Golding for advice on getting to sleep because he's ten times more keyed up than I. That, and he's never had a problem telling me what to do. His method, he says, is "from an Eastern tradition. I can't remember where it's from, but you can think of it as a yogic or Zen practice. When you go to sleep, think about everything you did that day. You relive your day in minutiae. It will calm you. It will turn off the madness."

I try it. I lie in bed and recap every event of the day. Woke up, probably around 6:45, tired as hell. Pulled up the window shade and looked at the sunrise over Lake Michigan. This sounds corny, but every morning, the lake is a shock, and I always have a brief, Calvinist moment when I wonder if I'm worthy of such a view. Like, am I Great Lakes material? Then, my robotic ritual: walk to coffeemaker, pick up pot, fill with four cups of water, pour said water into machine, take out filter, fill with five and a half spoonfuls of coffee, turn on. While brewing, ingest one stress vitamin, the kind with a picture of a candle burning at both ends (get it?) on the wrapping, open door, grab *Chicago Tribune* and *New York Times*, which I read, *Times* first, in unwavering order: arts section, business section, front page, editorial page, rest of front section, *Trib* gossip column (it's really gone to hell), and the TV column (still good). In which time I have had two cups of coffee, a bowl of cereal and glass of orange juice, and a third coffee when I got to the *Trib*. Checked email. Sent email. Took shower. Wrote a review of the new Tom Waits record. I'm fond of the ballads, so I wrote that I'm fond of the ballads. Which obviously takes one sentence to say, but I spent five hours stretching this into four hundred words. Then lunch—turkey sandwich. Did some dishes while listening to Ray Charles. Phone rang. It was Dave, a writer friend. We talked for over an hour, mainly about punctuation. He has big plans for the ellipsis. He's mad for ellipses. I tell him, yeah, I have similar affection for the parenthesis (but I always take most of my parentheses out, so as not to call undue attention to the glaring fact that I cannot think in complete sentences, that I think only in short fragments or long, run-on thought relays that the literati call stream of consciousness but I like to think of as disdain for the finality of the period). Dave is trying to decide whether he wants there to be a space before or after the ellipsis. He's unsure. Is the ellipsis approach powerful because of what is not said after the dot dot dot, or is it a cheap excuse for not being able to verbalize? Conversely, do we parentheticals want to communicate by cramming more in, thus slapping what we're not saying in between what we are, officially, saying? Or is it because we can't decide? After I hung up the phone I turned on the radio and a Randy Newman song was playing, and I thought, oh no, Randy Newman's dead. But he wasn't dead, some of his film music had just been nominated for an Academy Award. So that was nice, Randy Newman not being dead. Went for a walk on the lake, for maybe an hour. Read a novel for a couple of hours. Called my sister. Watched *Melrose Place*.

Miraculously, though, Barrett was right. By the time I get to what I cooked for dinner, I start to drift off. I'm drowsy. This is working. But then I remember the UPS man. I *hate* the UPS man! I am suddenly awake, seething. He's always bossing me around. Not only do I hate him because he's a bully, I hate myself for caving in. He scares me. So when he barks at me to take everyone else's packages—like I'm the postmaster general of the apartment building just because I work at home—I tend to acquiesce. So I'm always tripping over the other tenants' oriental rugs and Tony Robbins packages in my living room. The UPS man looks exactly like the late character actor J. T. Walsh but his voice is more sinister and clanging, an evil Gilbert Gottfried yelp. "Buzz me in! Meet me at the elevator!" he commands. No door-to-door, no please and thank you. No polite FedEx guy exit line like "Have a good one." I waited at the elevator ten minutes this morning, as he apparently delivered other people's packages. For a change. "Sign here!" he screamed, slamming his electronic pencil into my hand. I have heroic fantasies of someday having the guts to just jab it into his eye.

In the middle of this memory, I have gotten out of bed, turned on the light, and started pacing, mumbling under my breath about the *service* industry and that there's nothing more depressing than bad capitalism. And I realize that even for people who don't leave the house, Barrett's strategy will only work for those whose days don't include *some* incident that makes them mad enough to wake up. Until the world is rid of telemarketers, pit bull–owning neighbors, gas leaks, and George Will, this personalized update of the old counting sheep routine is not going to help. Because every day, no matter how cheerful, how innocuous, always contains within it some little speed bump of anger or hate, some wrong place, wrong time, hell-is-other-people moment of despair. Nighty-night.

DAY THREE: THE DOCTOR

I seek professional help from a doctor at the University of Chicago's sleep disorder lab—one Wallace Mendelsohn, professor of psychiatry and medicine. According to him, there are thirty or forty different sleep disorders. "Among the many causes of insomnia," he says, "is a condition called psychophysiological or conditioned insomnia."

I don't know if he's a good doctor, but because of his lifeless voice and dead-wood delivery, if his patients want him to help them get to sleep, all they have to do is sit him down and ask him to say a few words about his job. As he talks about rest and the patients he's cured, it hits me that I've never been rested. I have no idea what it feels like to wake up refreshed. I start feeling really sorry for myself and tears come to my eyes and I'm wondering what I'm missing so I'm pretty much ignoring everything the doctor says. Though he does get my attention when he tells me about a disorder called sleep apnea in which the patient can't sleep because of suspension of respiration—the nonsleeper can't breathe. This is treated by being hooked up to some Frankensteinian machine, sometimes for years. The cure sounds a thousand times worse than the problem: Congratulations, you're a cyborg! Later, I'll tell a friend about it and she says her father's on one and now he can sleep but her stepmother can't because the thing's so noisy. I don't cope so well with equipment. Am I up for attaching myself to a breathing machine when I haven't even gotten around to owning a toaster?

The doctor refuses to give me any personal advice, arguing that I'm not his patient. Maybe he holds out for the paying customers. I do manage to squeeze a few pointers out of him for "someone," maybe one of those psychophysio people, an ailment I'm interested in having because its treatment sounds so low-tech: "For that particular sub-group one of the things that can be helpful is to try to strip the bed and bedroom of any associations except for sleep and loving."

Loving? Somehow he makes that word sound so dirty.

That night I take Dr. Mendelsohn's advice and clear everything out of my bedroom, half of which contains my bed, the other half of which just so happens to function as my office. I will be precise, because this is science. I remove seventy-eight books, stacking them in front of the closet in the other room. I transport fifteen pens, a turntable, a transistor radio, a tape recorder, and twenty-three magazines. I take away dozens of scraps of paper (some of which were handily stored on and in the bed itself). I unplug the computer and the fax machine and lug them out. Clearing away all this dusty stuff takes two Kleenex-filled hours. Then I get into bed—in the nude because the stacks of books are blocking the closet where I keep my pajamas—and I think about what a mess the living room is and how I'm going to have to haul all that crap back in here tomorrow. I never get more than about thirty minutes straight of sleep, though somewhere in there I manage to have a dream in which my bedroom is empty because I got robbed.

DAY FOUR: THE INTERNET

Doctors and mothers and friends—so old-fashioned. So twentieth century. If I want an insomnia-free future, I must look to the future. To the World Wide Web. It promises so much.

I do a search on insomnia. The first page I find is sponsored by the National Institutes of Health. It posits the three main causes of insomnia are old age, depression, and . . . female gender. Well, no wonder I can't solve my little problem.

Then I log on to something called the Virtual Hospital at www.vh.org. In the insomnia advice section, one of its suggestions is "Don't engage in stimulating activity before bed. Examples include playing a competitive game of cards or watching an exciting program on television."

I vow to avoid exciting programs on television. Which means one thing: turn on *The Tonight Show*. Jay Leno's monologue features humor about airlines and Viagra and Linda Tripp. A skit called "Presidential Jeopardy" pits Abe Lincoln and George Washington against President Clinton, who scores big in the "Hooters Waitresses" category. Then one of those animal guys comes out. The conversation goes like this:

Jay Leno: These must be pretty endangered.

Animal guy: Yeah. They are.

I'm asleep before the musical guest comes out. This advice is working the best so far. I stay asleep for five whole hours. Does everyone know about this? That maybe this is the reason Leno's ratings are better than Letterman's?

DAY FIVE: A DAY WITHOUT CAFFEINE IS LIKE A DAY WITHOUT . . . I'M SURE I COULD COME UP WITH A GOOD ANALOGY BUT I'M JUST TOO TIRED

Consensus (or should I say conspiracy?): I haven't mentioned it until now because it was just too painful, but every last one of my sources—my mom, my friend, the doctor, the Web—advises against caffeine. Which is a problem in that I have been addicted to coffee since I was fifteen. I no longer drink nearly as much as I used to but still, my motto: *Sine coffea nihil sum.* Without coffee I'm nothing. So today, I'm planning on nothing. I go cold turkey, starting with a brisk pot of peppermint tea at 8:30. By 10:15 I'm splayed on the couch with a cardigan sweater wrapped around my eyes. My head throbs. The phone rings every fifteen minutes. One of the calls is from a telemarketer, who hangs up when I start to cry. At 12:38, I crawl over to the cabinet where I keep the coffee can and sniff its contents. I turn on the television and watch *North by Northwest.* You know you're in agony when it hurts to look at Cary Grant.

It is a very long day.

And guess what? It doesn't work. I'm awake all night watching the clock, waiting for morning, when I can make coffee. At five A.M. I tell myself "close enough" and suck down six cups before 5:15.

Now that reason is restored, I come to this conclusion: If there's anything worse than insomnia, it's taking advice about insomnia, especially from people who can sleep. Being up in the middle of the night is kind of nice actually. It's quiet and dark and the phone doesn't ring. You can listen to records and weirder movies are on TV. I've never known another life and now I'm not sure I want to.

One of my earliest memories is listening to my dad, in the middle of the night. He was awake. I was awake. I called him to ask for advice about doing away with insomnia but he didn't have any. He sees no need to fix it. I recited for him the exact sequence of his nightly wake-up routine, how from my room on the second floor I could always hear him turn on the buzzing kitchen light, open and close a cabinet, turn on the faucet, stir bicarbonate of soda into a glass, even the way the spoon sounded when he set it down.

"Wow," Dad said. "Did you hear my ears wiggle, too?"

Then he goes back to bed, but not back to sleep. In the middle of the night, lying in bed, he invents these machines I don't pretend to understand. The night before we spoke, he was up plotting out something called a spoke duplicating lathe, adding, "I feel sorry for all those people who slept through the night and didn't accomplish anything."

We are flawed creatures, all of us. Some of us think that means we should fix our flaws. But get rid of my flaws and there would be no one left. If I looked in the mirror someday and saw no dark circles under my eyes, I would probably look better. I just wouldn't look like me.

American Goth

I'M SITTING AT MY DESK, QUIETLY "MINDING MY OWN" AS THEY SAY IN THE RAP songs, when my torturer darkens the doorway. She drags me into a cramped bathroom, shoves my head under a faucet, shines a blinding light in my eyes, cinches my neck in plastic sheeting, and comes at me with scissors. She douses me with chemicals and makes me sit there, dehydrating under the plastic while the acid stings my flesh. And so, when I look up from my desk and see her standing there with the scissors, I shudder.

"Hi, Mom," I say. "Guess you think I need a haircut?"

My mother had been a hairdresser before my twin sister, Amy, and I were born. More precisely, she was a hairdresser in Oklahoma in the 1960s. That era is usually characterized as a time when men and women were letting their hair down, but in Oklahoma, they were spraying hair *up*; the beehive was enjoying a golden age. Since Mom gave up her career to take care of us, all that energy that used to go into whipping hundreds of histrionic heads into an architectural frenzy was focused on the two of us. And since we were as bald as pharaohs, she killed time while our hair was growing in by Scotch-taping bows to our newborn noggins. Her ardor for our appearance increased as we got older, and her attentions never stopped at the neck: There were clothes, there were shoes, even the dreaded accessories. Amy liked to think about such things, shop for such things. Unlike me, my sister did not threaten to call Amnesty International every time Mom wanted to give her a home perm. I was a bit of an embarrassment to my mother—all scuffed shoes and stringy hair and lint.

Once, when Amy and I were fourteen, the three of us were getting out of the car after a trip to the mall. The neighbor woman, who was out watering her yard, saw the shopping bags and asked what we'd bought. Amy showed off her new candy-colored sweater and her hoop earrings and hot pink pants. The woman congratulated Amy. She then turned to me, pointing at the rectangular bulge protruding from the small brown bag in my hand. I reluctantly pulled out my single purchase—a hardback of *The Grapes of Wrath*. My mother looked at the neighbor, rolled her eyes in my direction, and stage-whispered, "We're going through a book phase."

It's such a hopeful, almost utopian word, that word "phase." As if any minute "we" would suffer some sort of Joad overload, come to "our" senses, and for heaven's sake, do something about our godforsaken shoes. But the book phase never ended. The book phase would bloom and grow into a whole series of seasonal affiliations including our communist phase, our beatnik phase, our vegetarian phase, and the three-year period known as Please Don't Talk to Me. Now that we are finishing up the third decade of the book phase, we ask ourselves if we have changed. Sure, we still dress in the bruise palette of gray, black, and blue, and we still haven't gotten around to piercing our ears. But we wear lipstick now, we own high-heeled shoes. Concessions have been made.

Still, I have been called a curmudgeon by *Bitch* magazine. That's the image I'm cultivating. But truth be told, I'm not as dour-looking as I would like. I'm stuck with this round, sweetie-pie face, tiny heart-shaped lips, the daintiest dimples, and apple cheeks so rosy I exist in a perpetual blush. At five foot four, I barely squeak by average height. And then there's my voice: straight out of second grade. I come across so young and innocent and harmless that I have been carded for buying maple syrup. Tourists feel more than safe approaching me for directions, telemarketers always ask if my mother is home, and waitresses always, always call me "Hon."

So the last time I got my hair cut, I asked my hairdresser if he could make me look more menacing. I said I admired Marilyn Manson's new hairdo and could he make me look like that. And even though my hairdresser is German and everything, when he was done with me, I have never in my life looked so sickeningly nice. Is it too much to ask to make strangers nervous? To look shady and untrustworthy and malcontented? Something needed to be done.

I happened to hear about a group of goths in San Francisco who offer goth makeovers to civilians and then take them to a goth club to see if they can "pass." Goths, for those unfamiliar with this particular subculture, are the pale-faced, black-clad, vampiric types, with forlorn stares framed by raccoon eye makeup. The name derives, of course, from "gothic," a style, according to my dictionary, "emphasizing the grotesque, mysterious, and desolate."

I've always admired the goths. There's something brave about them. Something romantic and feminine and free—not to mention refreshingly honest. If the funny T-shirt slogans and crisp khaki pants of the average American tell the lie that everything's going to be okay, the black lace scarves and ghoulish capes of goth tell the truth—that you suffer, then you die.

So I called Mary Mitchell, a.k.a. Mary Queen of Hurts, and asked for a private lesson in goth. She told me to come to San Francisco and pack some black clothes and she and her team of expert goths would handle the rest.

Coming up with black apparel for the occasion wasn't particularly problematic for me. One might describe my closet as Johnny Cash once described his: "It's dark in there."

I reported to a Market Street address where I met the five members of my death-warmed-over beauty squad. I met Indra, a gorgeous blonde in a long velvet skirt; Terrance, dashing in a velvet smoking jacket; the tall, dark Monique; Elizabeth, in strappy black leather; and, of course, Mary, whose seven-inch patent leather heels would relegate her later on to dancing only to the slowest songs, for fear of tipping over. They all turned goth in their early teens and they are, as Indra puts it, "*so* in our thirties."

Prior to meeting Mary Queen of Hurts, I found her sadistic nickname entirely appropriate, as she assigned me "goth homework" to do before my arrival. The assignment consisted of going through a punchy little primer she wrote with Indra and Terrance which outlines the seven steps to "gothitude." Step number seven? Write goth poetry. One of my poems is a haiku about compost, which I wrote while pondering decay:

> *eggshells pulverized*
> *tossed into the rot of life*
> *toenails of the damned*

Step number six asked me to go through my records and pull out the darkest, saddest song and play it over and over again—though the darkest, saddest stuff in my collection is all old country music. So my goth soundtrack is Roy Acuff's godless, drunk-driving, car-crash number "Wreck on the Highway," in which "there was whiskey and blood all together, mixed with glass where they lay."

Before anyone breaks out the eyeliner, we all sit in a circle and go through my homework. The whole thing reminds me of graduate school seminars, except these people are smart and funny and have something interesting to say.

Step one of the guidelines is choosing a goth name. Indra says, "Most of us have changed our names to be something more gothic. A lot of people legally change their name. Live it!" According to Mary, "If you go into any of the goth clubs nowadays, you'll find a lot of spooky names—like Raven and Rat and Sage."

When I was pondering a good goth name for myself, I paged through my reference books on death and dying looking for something gruesome. Nothing felt right. Maybe it's because I came of age in the '80s and I've seen *Blue Velvet* too many times, but to me, the really frightening stuff has nothing to do with ravens and rats. The truly sordid has a sunny Waspy glow. Therefore, I tell them, the most perverse name I can think of is Becky. It turns out that by saying the magic word "Becky" I have suddenly moved to the head of the class, gothwise. As Monique puts it: "You are understanding the pink of goth. You've skipped a couple levels and you went straight to pink."

The group's consensus is that pink is the apex of expert goth—that newcomers and neophytes should stick with basic black but those confident enough, complex enough, can exude gloom and doom while wearing the color of sugar and spice. Indra argues that pink can be "an intelligent, sarcastic color," though Terrance says of experimenting with pink, "Proceed with caution. I can't warn you enough."

As if they need to warn me. It would never occur to me to wear pink, just as it would never occur to Michael Douglas to play a poor person. These, I realize, are my people. Simpatico. I think that's why, at that moment, I'm willing and able to do something with them that I was never able to do with my mom: namely, sit still while they poke and prod and paint me without complaint. I know I'm in the right hands when Terrance reassures me, "When we're done with you, no one will call you 'Hon.' "

And then, there's a magical moment when Indra applies the critical first layer of bloodless powder and foundation. When I see the transformation in the mirror—out, out apple cheeks!—I ask Mary if there's a word for this whiter shade of pale. She tells me, yeah, that I look "Laura Palmer dead."

It's an astonishingly slow process. Indra decides to make me up like the silent film star Louise Brooks, shading in concentric circles of eye shadow and then liquid eyeliner, which takes a full five minutes to dry. She agonizes over lipstick, applies a birthmark in the shape of a snake on my cheek. Then, they dress me. By the time they're done cinching up the corset and stabilizing my bustle, I'm in so many layers of black lace scarves and fringe and fishnet stockings that I could play strip poker for three weeks straight without baring my belly button.

The finishing touches are applied in a full-on pit stop. I sit in a chair and Monique curls my hair while Terrance fusses with my lipstick and Mary paints my nails black. All at once. I find I enjoy this loving, methodical attention. All these people are putting all this thought into how I look. They kept cooing, "You look great! You look fabulous! I looooove the snake!" I am so pleased with the results that I keep looking in the mirror and smiling. I smile so much that Elizabeth reminds me that, technically, a good goth is supposed to pout. But I'm too giddy.

Something occurs to me: What if all those years my mom wanted to do just this—sit me down and fiddle with my hair—not because she wanted to torture me or because she was embarrassed about how I looked or because she missed her job? What if she wanted to do this for me to show me that she loves me? If all along she was trying to give me the feeling I'm getting from these strangers?

I thought *she* was the oppressor and I was the victim, but it can be just as true the other way around.

At 10:30, it was time to go to the club. But after two hours of primping, I was tired. I asked them if they ever spend so much time doing their hair and makeup that they're too pooped to go out. They said that for this very reason, there's a goth rule: You have to stay at the club at least as long as it takes to get dressed up.

The club we go to is called Roderick's Chamber, cheerfully named for a character in Edgar Allan Poe's "The Fall of the House of Usher." Everywhere: blackness, leather, lace, frowns.

The first thing I notice about goth's public face is that, while the women are almost uniformly stunning, the men look, to a man, pretty stupid. There's a lot of jewelry and goofy cloaks and silly tights. And fellas, a word about jackboots: Ick. Indra tells me that if I want to check out a subculture with a hunkier class of men, I should look into swing dancing. "*Oh. Daddy. Oh,*" she says. What is she? Some kind of traitor? Maybe she's alluding to a more profound point. The character and charm of the women here emanates from the way they playfully stick it to the idea that women are supposed to be sunny and upbeat. But the men, adopting the accoutrements of medieval knights and Nazis, come across as little boys; they might as well be running around the dance floor shooting cap pistols at one another's G.I. Joes. "That's why my husband isn't goth," adds Monique.

The thing I love most about the goth club is how passive it is. Hardly anyone talks to anyone else. It is free of the normal social pressures to smile and interact and appear content. There's none of that getting-to-know-you pickup crap. In fact, the mood is antithetical to pickups; it's more like stay away. No one cares if you dance. No one cares if you don't. As someone who often dreads strangers, the antisocial nature of this social situation makes me feel communal and part of something—one of us. Like, hey, I hate talking to you too! The mutual disgust is completely liberating.

The whole point of coming here is to stare and be stared at. Someone walking in off the street might think, What's the fun in that? And the answer is, all the interaction, all the fun, all the real moments happen at home, when you're getting dressed, talking about how you'll look with your friends. The club is about being seen—which is so inferior.

At least my goths don't seem to mind being seen with me, though that may be more of a testament to their sartorial wizardry than to any assimilation skills on my part. Even I can see who the sore thumb is here. Like a scene straight out of *The Munsters*, all goth contempt is beamed onto the dance floor, where a happy blond Fawn Hall looka-like in acid-washed jeans is smiling the night away, oblivious. Compared to her, at least outwardly, I am as goth as a Cure album dipped in blood.

I'm a completely new person until I look at my watch right before midnight and realize I'm missing *Nightline*. I'm having a good time, but I don't really need elaborate costumes and nightclubs for an evening of gloom and doom: I'm perfectly capable of having a dark old time in my black pajamas watching the news. After the mandatory two hours, I hug my goths goodbye. They give me the kind of smiles professors reserve for their favorite students on graduation day, like they're proud of me for pulling this off, but they're just as puffed up about having done so much with so little. There should be diplomas for keeping that much eye makeup in place.

I hail a cab. Usually, I am a cab driver's dream—polite, small, non-threatening. Perhaps that is why cab drivers always talk to me. But tonight, I am Becky. I am goth. Not a word from the driver. Bless him, he keeps staring at me and my eye makeup in the rearview mirror, watching his back. She is menacing, he's thinking. I can tell. His fear pays off. I tip him extravagantly. So extravagantly that I blow my cover. He turns and gives me a look that says, "Thanks, Hon."

These pieces first appeared, often in different form, in the following: "Shooting Dad," "Music Lessons," "The End Is Near, Nearer, Nearest," "Take the Cannoli," "Michigan and Wacker," "What I See When I Look at the Face on the $20 Bill," "Thanks for the Memorex," "Drive Through Please," "Dark Circles," and "American Goth" on *This American Life* on Public Radio International; "These Little Town Blues" and "Chelsea Girl" in *GQ*; "Ixnay on the My Way" in *Salon*; "Your Dream, My Nightmare" in *Request*.

ACKNOWLEDGMENTS

Most of these pieces were shaped, contorted, pummeled, and harangued into viability by my hilarious and heroic editor, friend, and driving teacher Ira Glass of *This American Life,* along with producers Julie Snyder, Nancy Updike, and Alix Spiegel, and fellow lifer Paul Tough (Canadian). I'm also grateful for the editorial stylings of Cynthia Joyce at *Salon,* Jim Nelson at *GQ,* and Susan Hamre at *Request.* Many ideas and anecdotes herein were lifted from my former *San Francisco Weekly* column, edited by Bill Wyman. And considering there's no excuse for my pilfering of the previously private lives of my father, Pat Vowell, my mother, Janie Vowell, and my sister, Amy Brooker, they've been good sports. For their assistance and insights, I am indebted to Dave Eggers, Marion Ettlinger, Jim Fitzgerald, John Flansburgh, Nicole Francis, Marcy Freedman, Barrett Golding, Robin Goldwasser, David Gomez of the New Echota Historic Site, the goths (Mary Mitchell, Terrance Graven, Monique Motil, Elizabeth Reardon, and Indra Lowenstein), Nicole Graev, Nick Hornby, my guardian angels Greil and Jenny Marcus, Tony Millionaire, my late uncle John A. Parson, *Nightline,* David Sedaris, my agent Wendy Weil and her assistant Emily Forland, Ren Weschler and Sara Weschler. Honorable mention to David Rakoff, who over the course of this book endured my whining, Disney World, and my whining at Disney World. Finally, the scrupulous Geoffrey Kloske at Simon & Schuster was committed, can-do, and usually right.

Sarah Vowell IS THE AUTHOR OF *RADIO ON:*
A LISTENER'S DIARY, A CONTRIBUTING EDITOR FOR
THIS AMERICAN LIFE ON PUBLIC RADIO INTERNA-
TIONAL, AND A COLUMNIST FOR *SALON*.